CLUB
TREASURER'S
HANDBOOK

The Daily Telegraph

CLUB TREASURER'S HANDBOOK

TONY LEVENE
&
RICHARD BALDWIN

Published by Telegraph Publications,
Peterborough Court, At South Quay,
181 Marsh Wall, London E14 9SR

© Telegraph Publications/William Curtis Limited 1988

Typeset and designed by Litho Link Ltd, Welshpool, Powys
Printed and bound in Great Britain by Biddles Limited, Guildford and King's Lynn

British Library Cataloguing in Publication Data
Levene, Tony
    Club treasurer's handbook.
    1. Great Britain. Clubs. Financial management
    I. Title
    367'.068'1

ISBN 0-86367-360-0

Contents

Appendices

Introduction

There are tens and possibly hundreds of thousands of clubs, associations and societies in Britain. Each year thousands spring up and thousands collapse or fade away. No one knows the total and even the estimates of the numbers involved in sports activities ignore 'unofficial' teams.

Records kept by central, regional or local bodies that supervise and aid activities ranging from swimming to sewing and from gastronomy to glassblowing are notoriously inaccurate. And much the same can be said for local council lists of voluntary activities in their area. In the excitement of setting up a new club, members often forget to tell anyone. And when a club ceases to function, it is no surprise that often no one bothers to withdraw the name of the organisation from whatever list it may appear on.

Most sports and other activities have governing bodies which strictly regulate them. Few people will consider joining a serious club unless its activity is ultimately under the control of a national body. But there is no obligation to join any national or local body and no need to inform anyone else of a club's existence. Nor are there any laid down legalities.

But while this potential formlessness and lack of bureaucracy are attractive, they are also a danger. When a club is started, its founding members hope that it will prosper. Alas, many do not. They die a premature death not because their original aims were far-fetched, but because they lacked proper structure. And nowhere is this more notice-able than in the area of money.

Leaving aside sports and leisure clubs which are run by an employer or local authority, relatively few clubs can run their affairs without any reference to money. Even one where members pay their own way on a purely individual basis each time they embark on an activity still need the telephone or the post office to smooth communications.

Clubs that run their financial affairs on a haphazard basis run two risks. The first is that they will lose control of their affairs. An unpaid bill makes it less likely that you will get credit next time. But the second is perhaps more important: the risk of a dispute over money between members.

Many clubs are formed from the basis of individual friendships. Others cause friendships and even longer term liaisons to spring up. Clubs have a social aspect beyond any chosen aims. Arguments over money can and do wreck such friendships. A member may think that other members have pocketed cash. Equally, one or two members may consider they are subsidising the whole thing from their own pockets. Neither is conducive to the good running of a club. These money disputes do not have to be over large sums. Money is a strange thing. People can become equally upset over a missing pound as over a missing thousand pounds.

According to the Shorter Oxford English Dictionary, the word 'club' has two main definitions. The first is a weapon, thin at one end and thicker at the other. The second main entry includes defining a club as a combination, a social meeting, a clique, a secret society, an association of persons interested in some object.

The link between the two meanings of the word 'club' is not entirely clear although as far back as 1625, there is a record of the word 'club' being used in the sense of 'gathering together in a club-like mass'. There is a second connection between the two meanings. As we have seen, the difference between a club and other hitting weapons such as sticks is the shape. The club needs the substantial thick end for its ultimate purpose of hitting enemies. But it needs the slim end for its system of control. The social club is much the same. It needs a mass of members. But it also needs guidance from the thin end. And the thin end is the club committee, in particular – given the overriding importance of money – the club treasurer or finance officer.

The Club Treasurer's Handbook is obviously intended for club treasurers. But it can also be profitably read by other members of the committee and indeed by all the members of the club. Good club treasurers will be the first to admit that they can benefit from the ideas, encouragement and watchfulness of others. Few feel that they want to be in a position where they are the only people in the organisation who can understand money and the club's finances. This puts an intolerable strain on the treasurer who may at times be unable to function at full strength through illness, business commitments or family obligations.

The Club Treasurer's Handbook is a guide to best practice and not an accounting and legal textbook. Anyone involved with the finances of a club, society or association will have to judge when the size of their organisation reaches a level where professional help becomes necessary.

One thing all true clubs have in common is that any surplus or profit is applied for the best needs of the members. Applying that rule may mean employing professional accountants and bookkeepers on a full or part-time basis. But even when that does occur, it is the elected treasurer who finally has to carry the can. Even if negligence is ultimately proven against a professional, the club treasurer will, in the meantime, have had to endure the wrath of the members.

1 Club structure

A club is merely a collection of individuals who come together from time to time for certain purposes in common. The great majority of clubs start like this and retain this status throughout their lives. It is, in fact, a lack of status. For in the eyes of the law, a club remains a collection of individuals unless it forms itself into a company, a friendly society or a charity – legal structures which tend to be more suitable for the larger club.

A club can be run as a business. Many of the governing bodies of British sports are clubs but organised on more or less business-like lines. They sell tickets for events, they organise fund raising and sponsorship and they own assets such as land and equipment in the same way as a business. But what distinguishes a club from the normal business enterprise is that a club exists for the benefit of its members. The 'coming together' is in a social rather than a business context. It implies that all the members have rights to the use of the club facilities and that when members leave the club – on resignation, retirement or death – they cease to have any rights. Even if they have been instrumental in building up the assets of the club, they cannot take a share out of the club. The club carries on.

A CLUB AS A BUSINESS

Contrast this with a company running a normal business. It will have assets and earnings but they will be owned by the shareholders. Shareholders have a purely financial relationship with the company. The shares can be bought and sold and left to others in a will. Each shareholder is an individual. Even if a shareholder is an employee or director, the shareholding is not dependent on that person's continuing work relationship with the company – unless it is previously agreed.

If a limited company misjudges either its level of pricing or the level of demand, it can go into liquidation. That is bad luck on the people to whom it owes money as they are unlikely to get their money back or even a part of it. Limited company status allows businesses to take risks. If they fail, the shareholders are liable for no more than the total share capital – both paid and unpaid – of the company. Contrast this with the position of members of a club committee who are liable at law for any debts incurred in their names. And this liability is more than a legalistic device. Committee members can be held personally liable for damages as well.

The best known case is that of the committee of the Blackburn Rovers football club which today is registered as a company but which, at the end of the last century, was a club. The committee employed a builder to repair a stand. The builder was not good at his trade, the stand collapsed and several spectators were injured. They sued for damages and eventually the court found that as the committee members had appointed the builder, they were personally responsible for the damages. This view was upheld in the court of appeal and although the case took place a century ago, it still holds as a precedent.

Liability for debts

Indeed, in some cases, one individual in the club, possibly the treasurer or secretary, could be held personally and individually liable for debts if they personally gave a purchase order. A treasurer who books musical entertainment for a Christmas dance which attracts no paying customers will have to pay for the band either from the club reserves or from his or her own pocket. There have been cases of club treasurers threatened with personal bankruptcy due to club debts. There have also been instances where creditors have pursued one member of a committee that took a collective decision to purchase goods which were left unpaid because he was the only member of that body with sufficient personal assets to pay off the debt even though it had been a collective decision to purchase the goods. In theory, all the members of a club can be held liable if a project they have approved in a meeting remains unpaid. But in practice, it is obviously easier to take action for debt recovery against one or two people rather than fifty or one hundred club members.

Clubs which take no credit or only buy goods on credit that they can be certain to pay for do not run into this problem. But many organisations will need to take some risks. Risks can occur when the bar steward orders drinks. The club may be left with a dozen different exotic liqueurs in opened bottles. And when the club commissions a building there is the risk that it will be a white elephant or that it needs expensive modification.

A CLUB AS A COMPANY

There are ways that treasurers and other committee members can avoid taking personal risk. One way is by turning the club into a company. Setting up a company is easy to do as there are company formation specialists in many cities and especially in London, Cardiff, Edinburgh and Belfast where the Companies Registries are kept. Whether it is an advisable action is less easy to judge.

A commonly used form is the 'company limited by guarantee' also known as a guarantee company. In such a company, members do not contribute capital so there is no need to buy a share (although it may be necessary to do so if the company is wound up). If, after receiving professional advice, it is decided to set up an ordinary limited liability company, it would be good practice for the shares to be issued to individual members with the proviso that no member should have more than one share and that the share has to be sold at a preset nominal value if the member resigns. An alternative would be for all the shares to be held in trust for the members. The company's articles of association should make it clear that the assets of the club are not to be shared out among the members if the company is wound up. The normal course would be for the assets to revert to a national or local body covering the activity of the club.

For a company to attain such status can be inconvenient and costly. Statutory meetings have to be held once a year, returns have to be made to Companies House and accounts must be presented for filing in a consistent form. Accounts of a company have to be audited by an independent qualified accountant adding to the expense. In addition, there are various statutory annual costs associated with company status. Companies have to file annual accounts within a set period and these as well as other returns are available for public inspection. And of course there is the cost of setting up the company which can be anything from £150 upwards depending on complexity.

TRUSTEES

The second way of preventing individuals being sued for debts is to include a clause in any order which states that the creditor can only look to the club itself and not to individuals for recompense in case of problems. The clause should be stated prominently and clearly on each order. It is worthwhile coupling this approach with the appoint-ment of trustees. Trustees are normally club members who are not on the committee. Their role is to represent the club itself in any legal area. They become the club in effect.

The problem with this route – and one that does not occur when a club is formed as a limited company – is when the club is being sued for negligence. An example would be an injury to a visitor caused by a faulty water heater. The injured party could sue the trustees who would be personally liable. If they lost the case, they could ask the club to repay their costs and any penalties. The difficulty occurs if that expenditure is greater than the assets of the club. The individual trustee is then out of pocket.

But before going to the cost of rearranging the club's affairs into a company or appointing trustees, remember there is no obligation on anyone to provide your club with anything at all on credit whatever your legal status. For while turning your club into a company limits the liability of the shareholders to the capital of the company, suppliers may not wish to extend credit to a new organisation which they do not know especially one whose legal liability may be as low as £100. In the same way as the directors of companies are often obliged to give personal guarantees to suppliers and to the banks that lend their businesses money, you may find that at least some of your suppliers will insist on cash upfront or personal guarantees from committee members. Faced with a clause stating that creditors have to look to the club itself rather than any individual, many suppliers will either refuse to supply, demand a rigorous inspection of the club's financial record or simply insist on striking out the clause. After all, whatever they may think of your personal probity, they have probably been caught out by bad debts in the past and they do not want any unnecessary repetition.

Rules for a rule book

Whatever the legal status of the club, it will need clear rules and these rules must include provisions for a change in status. It is best to start out with a rule book that will not just cover likely eventualities but also act as a framework for changes in the future. If the club grows rapidly, it should have the rules to cope. Otherwise chaos ensues. Copies of model rules can usually be obtained from the national

organisation covering your activity. They provide a framework but they should be read carefully and changed where
necessary.

Financial problems can often be avoided by clarity in the
rules. Setting out the aims and objectives of the club in a
manner which can leave no doubt may well prevent club
officers committing the club to purchases which have no
real purpose. If a club is formed to play soccer and a
committee member orders a dozen rugby balls then he is
obviously acting outside the rules of the club and the club
cannot be responsible for any such debts.

It is as well to ensure that no financial decision – or no
decision over a certain value – can be taken by one person.
The rules should state that a sub-committee should be
formed for each spending area such as buildings and ground
maintenance, the bar and entertainments. The club
treasurer should serve on each of these sub-committees
along with two others. At least two signatures – again the
club treasurer should be one – must also be the rule on any
cheque issued by the club.

2 Treasurer's duties

Whether your club is formed from financially literate stockbrokers, accountants and tax lawyers or largely composed from those less sophisticated in matters of money makes no difference to the importance of the position of club treasurer. The financial affairs of a club cannot be decided by the membership as a whole. Unless the club has very few members, such a structure would be unwieldy in the extreme.

The management committee

Instead the membership must put its financial affairs into the hands of the management committee on which the treasurer sits as a matter of right. In this respect, the club is very much like a company. Unless it is very small, shareholders have to put their faith in a management structure.

Just as the board of directors of a company have a duty to ensure that the company prospers financially and is established on a firm financial footing, the management committee of a club has responsibility for the club's finances. Day-to-day financial decisions in a company are dealt with by the finance director. In a club, these will be dealt with by the treasurer who will report in the first instance to the management committee. The members can, of course, vote out the treasurer or the entire management committee in a way consistent with the club's rules.

The treasurer's position

There will be times when treasurers can act on their own without reference to the management committee, within guidelines issued by the management committee. Club treasurers will frequently have to make speedy decisions that may well involve a degree of confidentiality. The club may, for instance, have a policy of reducing or waiving fees from members who are in financial difficulties. The treasurer may have to decide on the limits of eligibility for such concessions and whether individuals fit into those guidelines. This is obviously work where both sides must keep complete confidentiality and where both sides of the transaction will be happier keeping dealings on a one-to-one basis. A treasurer may also be able to initiate transactions below a certain value without reference to the committee.

Club treasurers *must* ensure that their position and their duties are clearly laid down. The primary duty of the treasurer is to have control over the club's bank accounts. As such club treasurers are the servants of other members of the committee who are in a position either to raise funds or to spend cash. The club's rule book should lay down that there should be an office of treasurer and that the treasurer must be a signatory to any banking transaction. Cheques need to be countersigned and the rules should state that there should be a number of defined persons, any one of whom can sign along with the treasurer. One additional signature should normally be sufficient but a club may wish to insist on more if a cheque is over a certain value. The bank must be told of the exact rules and it would bear a responsibility if it paid out on a cheque or other withdrawal that was not drawn correctly.

The rule book should also lay down that there should be a finance sub-committee. Given the importance of money in the running of the club, the rules should make it clear that the finance sub-committee stands above other sub-committees such as that selected to run the bar. It is of course subservient to the full committee which in turn has to report to the membership as a whole. The treasurer and the secretary should be members of the finance sub-committee ex officio. The maximum practical size would be five persons although the finance sub-committee should be able to co-opt others when necessary.

THE CLUB SECRETARY

The club treasurer has many areas of responsibility. So too does the club secretary. On occasions, these will overlap and there could be confusion and possibly friction between the two office holders. Obviously, the treasurer's powers will be in part defined by the cheque-signing function. But questions of wage levels to staff such as groundsmen and bar workers could fall to either officer. In this particular case, a solution would be for the secretary to carry out all direct dealings with staff but within financial guidelines from the treasurer. That way staff know exactly where to turn with wage claims and other matters while the secretary cannot make arrangements that might be detrimental to the club's finances. Whatever is decided should be minuted so that it forms a precedent for future officers. Do not forget that the finance sub-committee is directly responsible to the committee which is answerable to the membership.

The treasurer's tasks

The principal task of the treasurer is to control the club's money and to account for it.

Club treasurers are in charge of arranging matters of taxation. Depending on the size and scope of the club 'taxation' could comprise any or all of the following: value added tax, national insurance, income tax including the collection of the tax from employees under the Pay As You

Earn system and corporation tax on profits including capital gains, whether or not the club has been formed as a company.

Treasurers must take charge of the bookkeeping function. In a large club, they might find it easier to sub-contract some of the keeping of the accounts books but in the event of a problem, the treasurer will have to take responsibility.

Although some large clubs are set up and run as businesses, the great majority are organised for the benefit of their members. And that means that the members are in overall control. They can unseat the treasurer and any other officer at an annual meeting and many clubs have rules which allow for an extraordinary meeting at any other time provided that a certain number or a certain percentage of the membership demand it. Members must have access to the membership list so that members can be circulated with demands for an extraordinary meeting. Many clubs will not be willing to hand out the list to anyone because it could be used for commercial purposes. Clubs should however be prepared to circulate any message falling within its rules to all members on behalf of a member or group of members willing to pay the costs involved. Communications are not the sole prerogative of the committee.

It is normal practice to give twenty-one days' notice of an annual meeting and fourteen days' notice of any other general meeting whether called by members or the committee. Committee meetings can usually be called at seven days' notice or less depending on the size of the committee and the degree of communication between committee members. Notices convening committee and sub-committee meetings can be less formal. Many clubs find it essential for the finance sub-committee to meet on a regular date in each month. Meetings need to have a certain number of members attending to be quorate. The rules should make the level for each form of meeting clear.

ANNUAL ACCOUNTS

Treasurers should send out the annual accounts with the notice of the annual general meeting. The ideal is for the accounts to be presented in three layers; the main figures highlighted to give an instant picture of the club's financial position, the formal accounts and detailed notes to the accounts. The treasurer's report accompanying the accounts – this is not a legal necessity but it ought to save time at the annual meeting and enable members to understand better what is happening to their money – should discuss the top layer of figures and describe why the club has made a profit or loss over the year and the year end level of the club's bank balances. The second layer is the formal accounts (see Chapter 5) while the third layer presents additional details such as expenditure on wages and a breakdown of sources of income.

Many clubs may not wish to supply the third layer to each member purely because of cost when few members are likely to be interested. If that is the case, it should be enshrined in the rules but most clubs will want these details displayed on a notice board or otherwise made available to interested parties before and during the meeting. In some clubs, members have the right to inspect the books at any time. That can often cause confusion. It is far better to give members the right – again as part of the club rule book – to inspect the club's finances on a certain number of fixed dates each year or at two weeks' notice on request. This also provides the treasurer with the incentive to keep the books up to date. But whatever the rules say, treasurers should always be ready within reason to explain the financial position of the club (bank accounts, spending and income patterns and the balance sheet position) to both members of the committee and ordinary members on an informal basis.

The treasurer is not only responsible for reporting what has happened to the club's money but should also ensure that the club has enough money to carry out its activities for the coming year. The general meeting is an ideal opportunity to tell members about the likely state of club funds over the next year. It is often useful to show details of planned income and expenditure for the forthcoming year. This is particularly important if the committee feels it needs to justify a subscription increase or if capital is required to spend on new or improved club facilities.

The treasurer also has a duty to tell the members subsequently if things do not go according to plan and steps need to be taken to avoid a financial crisis. Even in the smallest club with simple affairs, the preparation of an estimate of income, spending and cash balances (a cash flow plan) and the comparison of this with what actually happens are essential.

3 Bookkeeping

Bookkeeping is the most tedious yet the most essential task that the club treasurer has to perform. Keeping clear and easy-to-follow books serves two important roles – one forward looking and one backward looking. The forward looking purpose is that well-kept books enable the club to plan ahead. Unless you have a good idea of how well facilities have been used in the past and what their cost was, you will not convince donors, sponsors or indeed members to support growth plans. A later chapter describes capital planning and how to set out your thoughts when you are seeking cash for development. Without good records of the past, that task will be impossible.

The 'backward' function of bookkeeping is the need to maintain records for the Inland Revenue, HM Customs and Excise, your own members, regional and national bodies controlling your activity and possibly local government authorities. There is often one member in a club who is convinced that all the cash has been subverted to the treasurer's personal bank account. Good books can refute that slanderous suggestion.

At its most basic, bookkeeping involves a record of what money comes in and where it comes from and a record of what money goes out and where it goes to. Everything including paperwork such as receipts, invoices and bank statements should be dated, numbered (especially if several transactions take place on one day) and filed. Be prepared to keep all paperwork for a minimum of six years. Professional bookkeeping can be expensive and only in the biggest clubs where there is a full-time secretarial service will anyone other than the club treasurer undertake this task. It is worthwhile having an assistant treasurer who can deputise for you if you are away on business, holiday or absent through illness.

Set aside a regular time each week or month to take care of paperwork. Obviously, the amount of time you spend on it will depend on how active the club is and how many members there are. Discipline is the key to the task. If your club is of a size or a legal status where a professional audit is necessary, well-kept books will reduce the amount of time taken and so cut down the audit fee.

The books

Most clubs require a system no more complicated than a large cash book with several columns. You can get this from any good stationer who specialises in supplies for business. It is better to buy a book with too many columns rather than too few as you may wish to subdivide later some of your headings such as a separate analysis of bar food from bar drinks. Many club treasurers will find it tempting to use one of the very many programs which are available for home computers. Few clubs have the complexity of accounts that need full electronic treatment and using a computer can have drawbacks. Most members have more confidence in a well-bound cash book completed in ink. They can understand it and they can detect if any unauthorised change has been made. Equally, you may need to pass on the books to someone else who may not have access to a computer or one that uses the same system.

A typical small club would use one double page spread of a cash book per month. On one side, you will need to detail receipts – the cash that comes into the club. Headings on columns such as membership subscriptions, ticket sales, bar sales, hire of equipment to third parties, sponsorship payments and gifts will help you to analyse where your money is coming from. Although once in your bank account all money is the same, knowing where it comes from is vital for forward planning and spotting weaknesses. You will also need a column marked 'sundry items' or 'sundries' and space for detailing them as there will inevitably be items outside your main categories.

You do exactly the same on the other side of the page except here you detail expenditure. A typical club will spend money on food and drink, equipment, maintenance and upkeep but no two clubs are exactly alike so you will have to create your own headings. Again, you need a 'sundries' column. At the end of the first month of your club year, you add up all the columns and carry them forward individually to the next month. You then put all the following month's daily (or less often for a less active club) totals and add those to the carried forward figures to produce a new carried forward figure.

You also require a column on both sides headed 'bank account'. At the start of each month, you should indicate your bank balance on the income side. On the receipt or income side, you then list in correct date order all the payments made into the bank. On the expenditure side, you list all the cheques you have written and any other payments made. At the end of the month (or at any other time) you total all the payments in, do the same for all the payments out and subtract one from the other. If receipts are greater than expenditure, you have made a profit which you can add to the bank balance at the end of the previous month. But if it is the other way around, you will need to take the loss away from the figure you started with.

This figure may not accord with your bank statement because both credit and debt items may still be in the system. You should regularly check the bank balance shown in your books with that shown on your bank statement and identify the differences. Remember that it may take a week or longer for a cheque that you have made out to be paid in and debited from your account. If items are still absent one month later, however, make inquiries. This should occur but rarely. Again, regular checking and cross-referencing is an important discipline in keeping the books straight.

If you are registered for VAT, you will need a column on both sides showing the VAT elements in each transaction where this is necessary.

INTERPRETING THE FIGURES

By accurate recording you can analyse your club's finances month by month and heading by heading. You will know, for instance, if bar takings have fallen off suddenly and you will have to find a reason. It could be the weather, it could be light-fingered bar staff, it could be you are charging too much for drinks or a new more attractive drinking place has opened across the road.

It is normal for some months to produce a loss and some to show a profit. Membership subscriptions may only be due in April and October boosting these months. December will be a good month if you have a bar but you may need to pay for supplies in November and replenish in January. And both months are often quiet in the bar. Always try and find reasons for ups and downs. Seasonal variations are normal in most activities. Tennis and cricket thrive in the summer. Amateur dramatics do better when the nights draw in. If you can find no obvious reason for a change from the normal pattern of cash inflow, make further investigations. It is your duty to both the club and yourself and it applies whether the deviation from the pattern is upwards or downwards.

Using a bank

It is advisable to put all receipts through the bank and pay for all expenditure by cheque. That way, you have a permanent record kept by an independent third party of what is going on. You must never use your own bank account for this purpose although treasurers of small clubs have been known to ignore this rule. It raises the spectre of fraud even when – and this is true of over 99 per cent of such incidents – no fraud is intended. But even more importantly, it causes inefficiency. With the best will in the world, separating your own cash and your own bank charges from those of the club can be difficult. This may sound like labouring an obvious point but it is one that causes several clubs each month to end up in trouble.

Banks vary in their attitudes to club accounts. All high street banks welcome new business, especially from clubs with a substantial cash flow. Before signing up, find out their attitude to charges and whether they will impose any extra charges for handling substantial sums of coins and notes or the large amounts of small cheques and postal orders that can befall clubs where a substantial part of the membership pays subscriptions by post. As you would expect, you will find that there are variations between banks. Equally, there are often major differences between branches of the same bank. It may all depend on the attitudes of the local bank manager.

There is also a form of interest paying account with a cheque book which is worth considering if the club regularly issues large cheques or if the club is involved in a major project such as building a clubhouse. And that is the High Interest Cheque Account, known in the banking business as a HICA. This form of account is available from high street banks as well as from a number of less well-known financial institutions. To obtain the full benefit of the interest bearing part of a HICA, you will need to have a high minimum balance – usually in the region of £1,000 – and restrict the number of cheques you write each month as some HICAs levy a charge for each cheque over a certain number each month or quarter. That number might be as low as one or two per month. The rules for the various HICAs are constantly changing and some research will be needed to find the one that fits your club's own profile the best. Unit trust and banking group Save & Prosper, itself a provider of HICAs, publishes a guide to the maze (from S & P Consumer Services, Romford RM1 1BR) which is rated accurate and unbiased.

One unsung advantage of a HICA is that the restrictions act as a form of discipline on the club treasurer. Payments in and out tend to become more regular. You can also operate any of the above forms of interest bearing accounts at the same time as the standard bank current account. You will have to move one cheque a month from your high interest to your current account.

It may be false economy to move banks just to chase a few more pounds of interest if you have a good relationship with your present bank manager. Banks recognise they have to be competitive with one another and few banks allow themselves to be grossly out of line with their customers for very long. Banks have a formal and legal duty to their customers. Amongst other requirements, they must keep accurate accounts and should not pay out items that are not backed up by the correct signatures. But you have a less formal duty which is one of not abusing the banking system by moving accounts every month or so. After all, many bank managers try actively to help club accounts even though most are not very profitable for them.

BUILDING SOCIETIES

It is also worth considering building societies. Many have special treasurers' accounts which enable clubs to receive interest without any tax deduction although in some cases the rates paid are so low that a club would do better with a standard account even with the deduction of tax.

Several of the largest building societies have chequebook accounts which pay interest. Some work in exactly the same way as bank accounts offering exactly the same facilities. Others operate in conjunction with a high street bank working a 'cash sweep' which allows you to keep all of your funds above a certain level (usually around £300 to £400) in an interest bearing building society account. Very small clubs which only need to issue cheques occasionally might find that they can use a standard building society account with a passbook. When cheques are needed, the society can issue them over the counter in return for a correctly drawn withdrawal notice signed by the correct number of signatories. This does, however, mean that you have to visit the society whenever you want a cheque. Some societies may be prepared to offer you a special deal if a large number of your members open personal accounts. Don't forget that your membership list is always worth something to outside bodies.

For many clubs, operating a cash book and a bank account may be the limit of the necessary bookkeeping. But it is as well to add a few checks and balances. You should always give a receipt for all cash received. If the membership secretary has collected subscriptions from thirty members at £10 each, then the £300 should be acknowledged with a receipt that spells out the split between cash and cheques. Use a duplicate book so that a permanent record can be kept on the carbon copies. Likewise, you should keep documentary evidence to back up every cheque you pay out. Photocopy all invoices. It cannot be stressed too often that being club treasurer is not a personal fiefdom or a job for life. The easier the system is to operate if you have to pull out, the better you have carried out your task. Don't forget that the monthly figures will form the basis of the annual accounts which will be audited either by members of the club (if it is small) or by outside auditors from a firm of accountants for bigger clubs.

Most clubs deal on a cash basis. They offer no credit as most of their 'goods and services' such as food, drink and sports facilities are instantly consumed. A few clubs, especially those involved with promoting an unusual sport or those whose purpose is religious or political as well as leisure, may send off goods against orders which are not accompanied by cash. The cash book system cannot cope with this as essentially it records transactions which are complete – real money has gone in or out of the bank. You need a sales day book. Most of your customers will be occasional so you will not need to worry about long-term accounts. The easiest system to use is an invoice book with a duplicate, obtainable from any good stationer. Send the tear-out top copy to the customer and keep the second numbered and dated copy in the book. Make it clear that you expect cash within a set period: 30 days should be the longest. When payment is made, simply indicate the fact on the duplicate leaf and then enter it into the cash book as though it were a cash transaction received on that day. Regular inspection of the invoice book will indicate if there are any customers who owe your club money.

You may wish to back this up with a more formal record of invoiced but unpaid for sales. Purchase a sales book which should record in successive columns on one side of the page the date of sale, the name of the purchaser, the invoice number, the amount, the VAT (if applicable) and the invoice total. On the other side of the page, record the date on which the invoice was paid, the amount paid, the VAT paid, any discount (so that the amount paid and the amount invoiced can be reconciled) and any amount still outstanding. If there is an amount still to pay, enter it as a new line on the amounts outstanding side of the page. Remember that under most VAT accounting systems, you are liable to pay VAT that you have invoiced whether your customer has paid or not. There are, however, new rules for smaller businesses which allow them to account for VAT on a cash basis. This may be of some help to clubs. Chapter 13 on VAT planning has further details.

It is generally not worth allowing goods worth less than £10 to be sent out without payment. You can encourage prompt payment by offering a small discount or waiving postage charges if you have a cheque back within a short period. Operate such a system strictly but always look at the date on a postmark and the class of stamp used before rejecting any customer for a discount.

THE PETTY CASH BOOK

If only a minority of clubs use or need any form of sales invoicing, most clubs and all small clubs require a petty cash book. This records that host of small items which cannot be paid by cheque such as a fiver to a pensioner member who helped tidy up after the children's Christmas Party to the cost of a bottle of liniment for the Extra 'B' team. You will need to impose a strict limit on what counts as petty cash – perhaps £5 or £10 – otherwise all your accounting methods could become subverted. You must too insist on a detailed receipt for all monies spent. It is also essential to obtain a signature if anyone takes money from the petty cash box to make an urgent but small purchase. They should also return any change.

The best way of dealing with petty cash is to take cash out of the bank on a regular date each month, the amount based on past experience. If there is no past experience, start off with three times the maximum petty cash item value. So if you have imposed a ceiling of £10, start off with £30. There is nothing magic in this figure of three times. It is merely a convenient starting place so that you can see how things go over the next months by which time you will know whether the figure needs to be higher or lower. As soon as you take the money out of the bank, enter a debit item in the day book with reference 'petty cash'. You will not then enter any of the items bought for cash in the cash book as you would then be debiting the money twice over.

In the petty cash book, you can record each item as it is purchased either in one column or – if you find you need to carry out a lot of small item purchases for cash – in a number of columns headed variously 'petrol', 'postage', 'laundry' or whatever else suits you. That will help you analyse spending. You need to show any VAT paid out where this is applicable as you can still reclaim the tax. You must also show the date, the number of the receipt that was obtained and the petty cash voucher which authorised the purchase. Think of the petty cash book as a miniature version of the full cash book except you are not recording your bank balance with each transaction but the amount of cash in the petty cash box. Your credit items will be the cash from the bank once a month or however often is thought appropriate, plus the return of any change when you have given out cash before the item is purchased. Petty cash and petty cash boxes have a habit of disappearing – so be careful!

Summing up

There are a number of benefits from sound book and record keeping. Two of the most important are that the production of the annual accounts and the execution of the annual audit is made much simpler and that the treasurer of even the smallest club can plan and monitor its finances.

The annual accounts, which will usually comprise a profit and a loss account and a balance sheet show how successful the club has been over the past year in controlling the club's assets and cash (see Chapter 5). And a successful club means a successful treasurer.

4 Subscriptions

How much is charged for membership itself and how much for the activities of members may well depend on the expenditure pattern of the club. A club that raises large amounts of money through the sales of drink and the provision of gaming facilities such as bingo and fruit machines or the hiring of tennis courts will be content with a low initial subscription as it hopes to gain from a large number using its facilities. The same might well apply to team games where each member of a team is expected to pay each time they play. If the club wishes to raise £88 every time its soccer pitch is used, then there should be a clear rule – £4 a head or no game.

It is all a question of judging the proportion of fixed costs in the overall expenditure pattern. If a club exists to organise tennis players who use courts in a public park for which they pay on an individual basis following an agreement with the local council, the level of fixed costs is low. No land is owned so even low overheads such as postage and telephone bills should be in proportion to the numbers wanting to play. Here expenditure is closely linked to demand. The club treasurer will not notice too much difference in the club's finances whatever (for example in the case of tennis) the weather does during the season.

Equally, there are other clubs where costs are fixed, bearing no relationship to demand. Take a club devoted to the showing of pre-war railway films. It may have to sign a long-term agreement with a local cinema and it will certainly have to hire the films and pay for them well in advance. The costs are the same whether one person or one hundred people turn up. Here there is a strong case for a high rate of subscription and perhaps free or nominal charges for entry. That way, the treasurer can give the committee the confidence to plan a programme. High subscription levels will deter many members. But a club with high fixed costs can be run on low membership fees as long as there is high usage of facilities. This tactic can also work if the club has built up financial reserves which can cushion any temporary problems. But there is a distinct risk – especially for the newly-formed club.

Clubs may wish to set out varying levels of membership such as junior, retired, country or playing. Each category may have their own subscription rate and their own facilities. The rules should be crystal clear on the payment of membership subscriptions. The levels will normally be set by the club committee, guided by the treasurer and presented for approval to a meeting of members. Whatever the level of subscription, the rules should make it very clear that no subscription can be refunded under any circumstances. It is usually worthwhile making that clear on membership cards by repeating the rule. It should also be evident from the rules just what membership does cover. As the club grows, it can have an important effect on the payment of VAT.

Fixing the rates

The following questions and suggestions will help treasurers and club committees in fine tuning subscription levels.

* Are subscriptions an important part of the overall income of the club?
* Should there be a low subscription level and charging for all facilities or a high level of annual fees and free or low cost facilities?

* Is the purpose of the club primarily social – eating, drinking and talking? If so, a low level of subscription is called for. You are effectively competing with the public house which charges no admission fee.
* Do members provide their own equipment?
* Do members want to 'pay as they play'?
* Is regular upkeep necessary?
* What is the level of subscriptions and service at rival clubs in the area?
* Is there a waiting list for the club? If so, you could use market forces to push up the levels of subscription.
* Will the level of subscription have an effect on outside providers of cash such as a grant giving body or a bank?
* Are your costs the same if one member turns up or if one hundred attend an event?
* Is your activity one that lends itself to family use?
* Is there a purpose in having different levels of membership such as family, junior, senior citizen? Some clubs have social membership which allows use of the bar but not of sporting or other facilities.
* If you are providing a high level of free facilities, will it aid club funds to have special membership categories to encourage use of the facilities in otherwise quiet periods such as weekday mornings or late at night? Remember that you may have to pay staff overtime.
* Is offering life membership, perhaps at five or ten times the annual rate, worthwhile?
* Should you offer reduced rate trial membership for a few months, or should you reduce the fees for members who bring in fresh blood?
* Is it worth offering a discount to members who renew by standing order, saving you the trouble of chasing them?
* Have you considered corporate membership whereby anyone who works for a local company is automatically a member in return for a lump sum donation from the employer? Such a deal could be part of a sponsorship arrangement (although it could raise tax problems for the employees).

5 Club development

Many clubs start as small self-supporting organisations. They often meet once a month or once a week in premises or on grounds that are hired for the duration of the meeting. Members contribute cash at each meeting and this money pays for the hire of facilities on that occasion. Membership fees cover such facets as the posting of details of club activities to members and arranging matches and other events with rival clubs. The great majority of clubs never need go beyond this. If membership numbers fade in a club despite all the best efforts of members, the club treasurer and the other committee members may decide to throw in the towel. The club simply fails to reappear when the next season starts.

But a number of clubs will have the ambition to grow. Others have already progressed beyond the minimal level and have greater goals in sight. Any club treasurer who wishes to join them needs firstly to recognise three important truths.

1. To go beyond the first level means adopting a business-like attitude. That means keeping financial records in a comprehensive and up-to-date system although that need not mean especial complications or expense. Clubs do not see themselves as businesses, however. They rely on the voluntary ethos and they have social and non-profit making objectives.

2. In general clubs have little cash in reserve. There is no fat to cushion a wrong decision.

3. Clubs compete in the leisure market against all manner

of opposition ranging from the professionally-run and immaculately-presented commercial leisure centre to the trend towards a greater variety of home entertainment via television. Remember that the cash and time that an individual can devote to leisure can only be used once.

This chapter deals with the financial aspect of development.

FINDING THE MONEY

There are two main methods of raising cash for expansion. You can tap the enthusiasm and energies of the members or you can raise a loan or find a body that is willing to give you a grant. The former method may not only involve members dipping into their own pockets but also, and more productively, spending time and effort in raising funds from non-members. The bank or grant route demands a more formal application and that may prove just as difficult as using your members as a resource. They will not only need persuading at the outset but also regularly thereafter as many will not understand that large projects can take time.

Accounting and budgeting are essential both on a day-to-day basis and as the foundation for cash raising. This chapter will explain how to develop the basic records discussed in Chapter 3 into cash flows for capital projects as well as the profit-and-loss accounts and balance sheets. Not all are appropriate for every club and very large clubs will obviously seek professional accountancy help. But the great majority of clubs are likely to carry out their accounting along the lines of the 'do-it-yourself' methods described in this chapter.

Club treasurers and committees need to take action that is both forward looking and defensive. The forward-looking action is to prepare realistic plans for expansion backed by cogent figures based on the past and a conservative estimate of the future. The defensive aspect is to ensure that the present club structure is built on solid financial foundations. As the lack of foundations effectively stops all future building work, it is as well to consider what can be done in this respect first.

There must, of course, be firm controls over all spending. Clubs that allow anything other than a petty cash item to be purchased without the authorisation of the committee run serious risks. Accounts showing the cash-flow position should be available for each committee meeting and those meetings should be no less often than once a month. Sensible clubs, clubs that survive the first enthusiasms and grow, do this anyway.

Procedure for development

The next stage is to prepare a plan for expansion. Central to any development is a business plan that extrapolates current and expected trends. Creating such a plan will be much easier if the day-to-day bookkeeping has been well maintained. The plan will set objectives for the club over the near future and also over a longer period such as three years. It is best to do this well in advance of any thoughts of major expansion so that you can check just how accurate your budgeting and planning are. You can compare your actual results with your forecast and analyse any differences. You can then take whatever corrective action is necessary to ensure that the club's objectives are met.

The business plan for the club need not be complicated. In fact, it should not be as you will probably have to show it to many members who are not necessarily well versed in matters financial. It is a statement about the objectives of the organisation, where it is going and how it is going to get there, emphasising financial aspects. The plan itself will usually consist of a minimum of six sub-sections as follows.

1. The summary.
2. The business.
3. The market.
4. The management.
5. Financial analysis.
6. Action plan.

The committee should be responsible for producing the business plan although professional advisers can often provide help if only to read through and comment on the final draft.

It is essential to have an accurate idea of the cost of any development together with the timing of payments. This is sound business sense anyway but can be even more important for a club which is likely to have scant or no reserves to help it over cash flow imbalances. To take a simple example, if you have to pay out £2,000 on December 1st, you may need to make special arrangements as the cash from the Christmas and New Year spending at the bar and your New Year's Eve Ball will not be in the bank. You must either raise an overdraft or a short-term loan from a bank or arrange for the payment to be deferred (or try to borrow cash from a wealthy member!). Knowing about your likely cash flow will enable you to identify the problem ahead of time and deal with it in a calm fashion.

Inflation is lower than it has been for some years but it is still a vital factor. You will need to build inflation into your financial estimates for the future. It is worth remembering that the figures given for inflation relate to a 'basket' of goods and services. They include a multitude of factors such as mortgage interest, admission costs to entertainment and the cost of a pint of beer. At any given moment, the rate of inflation in a specific area such as construction – for example if the project is to build a new pavilion – will be greater or lesser than inflation measured by the RPI (retail prices index). Recently wages have been growing faster than prices in general. So if your project is one that will use a lot of labour, build in a higher-than-normal rate of inflation.

As well as inflation, it is as well to build in a margin for the 'worst case'. What happens if your new facilities only attract 10 per cent more business instead of the 50 per cent that other clubs have experienced when they have carried out similar developments? And what happens if the costs run over the estimate by 20 per cent? Any new venture is a risk but the experience of others is a good yardstick to start with. You need to calculate how far you can deviate from your budget before the development becomes totally untenable. If that margin is small, say 5 per cent, you may feel that the risk involved is just too much. Almost any slippage would put the club out of business. It is best to carry on as you were. Obviously, if the margin is 50 or 100 per cent, you can allow for far greater leeway: your risk is reduced.

How accurate are your estimates?

Features that can cause you to add or subtract from your estimates in best and worst cases can be summed up under the heading of sensitivity. Ask yourself questions based on the following models. It is assumed that the club wishes to build a new clubhouse with luxury facilities to replace the tatty one presently in use.

1. You have made the following statement. 'If the facilities are improved, we intend to increase the annual subscription from £35 to £50. And as the club will be larger, we expect 50 new members.' How sure are you of those figures? How do the new costs compare with what is available elsewhere in the area? What will be the effect of a standstill or reduction in membership numbers?

2. You have assumed that the loan the bank will give you will be at a variable rate of interest linked to the bank's

base rate. There has been a wide range of interest rates over the past ten years. What happens if they go up?

3. At present you receive sponsorship from a local pizza restaurant. But after your club has built a new clubhouse that provides food, you will be in direct competition. Have you discussed this with the sponsor?

4. Will any additional tax complications outweigh the benefits of expansion? The project could affect the entire tax position of the club. If the new facility was open to the public, then the club may start to carry on a taxable trade as a result. Tax allowances on new capital assets are usually extremely limited and in the case of a members club which is not paying tax, there can obviously be no allowances whatsoever. There is no tax relief on the cost of the building itself (except in the event of a building in an enterprise zone) and any other capital spending will attract only a relatively low rate of tax relief known as 'a 25 per cent writing down allowance on a reducing balance basis'. And there is also the possibility of slipping into the VAT net. But it is also true that tax losses can be constructively employed. It is best to take professional advice on the tax aspect, especially if any deviation from your plan would be likely to put pressure on your cash flow.

Presenting the finances

If you can live with the risks, then it is time to look at the rewards. Prepare a best case scenario. This is useful as a target for members particularly if they are giving their own time for building work or fund raising. You, or one of your members, might have access to a computer with spread sheet software. This will enable you to produce a whole range of forecasts from the basic data quickly and easily. Figure 1 below sets out a basic and very simplified cash flow forecast for the development project. The headings have been left blank with the exception of the most important areas of expenditure and income. Create as many headings as you find necessary and include all items such as loans and repayments. At the end of each month, the bank balance brought forward, spending and income are balanced off to produce the end-of-month bank balance which serves as the starting point for the next month's calculations. In our example which covers ten of the twelve months in the year, one month has been left blank. This is the month that the club is closed for seasonal reasons. Some clubs will find that there are more inactive months. Others will have none.

CASH FLOW FOR THE PROJECT

If you are trying to project forward to forecast the effect on cash flow of a new project, it is best to set out a new cash flow statement just showing how you envisage the balance between extra income and extra expenditure that the new project will bring. You can then include this as a final figure which adjusts the cash flow you expect from the club's existing activities. If you have calculated correctly, you will see whether the club can stay viable when the project is under way or if – as has happened to both professional sports clubs and small local societies – the project for expansion brings down the club.

Having established the project is viable, try to set out monthly cash flow statements for the first year and quarterly figures for at least the next two years incorporating the new project into the existing activities. The level of detail will obviously depend on the needs of individual clubs.

Once you are sure that cash flow, together with any overdraft or other loan facilities that you have arranged, can cope with the project, the next stage in presenting a case either to a bank, a grant-making body or to your own members is to show the effect on the annual surplus you expect to make. Again, if your books are up to date and show a good degree of analysis, this should not be too

Figure 1
ADDITIONAL CASH FLOW FOR A PROPOSED NEW CLUBHOUSE BAR AND RESTAURANT

CASH FLOW FORECAST

PROJECT: NEW CLUBHOUSE BAR AND RESTAURANT

Cash Balance	Month	Income				Expenditure		
		Loan	Grant	Increased Subscription	Cash Receipts	Building	Cash Payments	Loan Repaid
£		£	£	£	£	£	£	£
—	1	4,000	2,000			5,000	1,000	
1,000	2			2,000		1,000		
2,000	3				2,000	1,000		
—	4	4,000				5,000		1,000
2,000	5		2,000					
1,000	6					1,000		
1,000	7	4,000	2,000	2,000		6,000		2,000
	8							
5,000	9				4,000			
1,000	10	4,000				5,000		3,000
1,000	11							
1,000	12							

Cash receipts would include:
1. Bar takings.
2. Restaurant takings.
3. Additional use of existing facilities.
4. Interest on cash raised from members and other sources (interest-free loans etc.).
5. Other receipts.

Cash payments would include:
1. Running costs (staff etc.) caused by the new project.
2. Other expenses (rates etc.).

Subtract the total of the payments from the receipts. In some months, especially the early months, the resulting cash flow figure could be negative. That is to be expected in any new project as you are unlikely to make money from the first day. See what effect that has on existing cash flow. Look at the cash flow you have prepared to illustrate the worst case and reconsider how much sensitivity you need to give that possibility. You can only go ahead with the project if the club has enough money of its own or can raise enough from elsewhere to pay for the new works.

difficult. Figures 2 and 3 show how to set out basic accounts for the year. The same formula can be used to show figures projected forward. Always mention the fact that these projected forward figures are unaudited projections. They are intelligent guesswork, nothing more, nothing less. And remember that when presenting figures from a year that has just passed to the members, it is customary to show the previous year's figures on the same basis for the purposes of comparison. The committee's report to the members should also include comment on figures that are grossly out of line from one year to the next.

Figure 2
CLUB PROFIT AND LOSS ACCOUNT FOR THE YEAR TO DECEMBER 31

INCOME	£
Income from membership activities	
Subscriptions	2,000
Donations	3,000
Income from non-membership activities	
Car boot sales	500
Hire of premises to non-members	1,000
Bar profits	8,000
Christmas dance surplus	200
Midsummer ball surplus	1,000
Sale of club T-shirts surplus	500
Profit on lottery	3,000
Interest on bank account	100
Total income	19,300

EXPENDITURE	£
Bar staff	5,000
Rates	500
Interest paid on loan	1,000
Repairs to equipment	400
Improvements to premises	2,000
Publicity	500
Transport	1,000
Total expenditure	10,400

Excess of income over expenditure	£8,900
Previous surplus brought forward	£18,100
Surplus to carry forward to next year	£27,000

Your members may also appreciate a balance sheet (see Figure 3 below). A bank or grant-giving body will certainly need one. A balance sheet sets out the total wealth of the club and shows how it is financed. It is effectively a snapshot taken on one particular day so it must be stressed that anything that has happened since the balance sheet date will not be included. However, it is customary to detail any major 'post balance-sheet' items. Again, it is normal practice to include the previous year's figures for the purpose of comparison.

There are a variety of ways of setting out a balance sheet. Items may not always appear in exactly the same place. But the basic idea is to show the assets: cash, property, motor

Figure 3
XYZ SPORTS CLUB
BALANCE SHEET AS OF DECEMBER 31

	£
Fixed assets	
Property	25,000
Cars	2,000
Equipment	3,000
Current assets	
Cash with bank	1,000
Stock	3,000
Debtors (money owed to club)	500
VALUE OF ASSETS	34,500
Less: current liabilities	
Short term loans	4,500
Creditors (money owed to others)	3,750
NET ASSETS	26,250
Financed by	
Long-term development loan	8,000
Grant (interest free)	5,000
Members' funds	13,250

vehicles, equipment, stock such as food and drink and debtors (money owed by others), and the liabilities: short-term bank loans and creditors (money you owe others).

Net assets

If you subtract liabilities from assets, you arrive at a figure known as net assets. Clubs where liabilities exceed assets are probably heading for financial trouble. Often short-term assets such as cash and short-term liabilities such as money you owe that must be paid within a short time to suppliers are shown separately as this shows how much there is 'in the bank' to meet the club's immediate needs. If short-term liabilities exceed short term assets, this is a very important warning signal to the committee. It tells the club they could be in financial difficulties.

You then need to show how the net assets are financed. In most clubs, it will be a mixture of long-term loans from banks and national bodies covering your activity, repayable grants and 'members' funds'. Members' funds are exactly what they say. If all the borrowings were repaid and all the goods bought on credit paid for, members would be left with certain assets such as cash or property. In theory, those remaining assets belong to the members. This is the ultimate in bottom lines if the club hits trouble. It is also the starting point for expansion. A bank would be far more willing to lend £1,000 to a club with members' funds of £10,000 than to one which only has £500. In effect, members' funds represent all the profitable activities of the past, less past loans and the interest payable on them.

If you are considering a major project, do not eschew outside help from a bank manager or accountant. They may not only have experience of other similar projects but they are also able to look at your plans with the eye of an outsider. Badly thought-out expansion plans based on over-optimistic forecasts is a major cause of the failure of many clubs, societies and companies.

6 Sponsorship

Sponsorship of sports, the arts and other cultural events and of charitable organisations is nothing new. Insurance companies and banks have long been backing sport, especially cricket. Horse races are named after companies that put up prize money. The sports and cultural world gets the cash, the companies get the publicity and increasingly the use of sporting and cultural facilities to entertain clients and staff.

Most sponsorship has been from national organisations and carried out at national level where the attraction of television coverage is often irresistible. Sponsorship can occasionally misfire, however. A razor blade maker pulled out of cricket sponsorship when its market research showed that it had become better known for cricket than for shaving accessories. The sponsorship of sports events by tobacco companies has frequently been criticised as a method of getting around the banning of cigarette advertising on television. And there was the brewery that decided to sponsor an evening's entertainment for delegates at a trade union conference. It put on its normal run of blue comedians with their near-to-the-knuckle sexist and racist versions of humour. The union had just spent hours discussing sexism and racism and the evening ended in a near riot, ensuring poor publicity for the brewery. The union in question consisted of journalists. But in general, sponsorship has worked well for both sides. The disasters are rare and when a major event comes onto the 'sponsorship' market, companies fall over each other in the rush to add their name to it.

Companies queue up to sponsor national events, the only discussion is the terms of the cash support and what they get back from it. Sponsorship at the local level is far less common. To a substantial extent, this is due to local clubs and societies failing to sell themselves as hard as they might. At the parish pump, both local and the regional offshoots of national and multinational companies need to be coaxed. You have to convince them of your value to them. It is no use simply writing to companies asking for sponsorship cash, you have to sell yourself positively.

Remember that sponsorship is different from a donation. You could ask for donations or pure patronage to prevent your club going out of existence with an approach designed to tug at the heart strings. That is less likely to work with approaches for sponsorship. For sponsors hope that what your club stands for will rub off on their concern. They are looking for success. If your group's operatics are the worst for a hundred-mile radius or your club's top hockey team lets in a minimum of ten goals each match, your work is that much harder. You will have to convince the would-be sponsor not just that the cash will enable your organisation to perform much better but that it will bring them positive results in the shape of better business. They also want a clean image. If the social side of your club regularly ends up in a drunken brawl that gets reported in the local newspaper, no one will want to know. Sponsor and sponsored have to mesh with each other. It is a two-way deal.

WHAT IS IN IT FOR THE SPONSOR?

You will be dealing with people who may never have thought of sponsorship or any other form of support for local clubs. Potential sponsors will ask two questions once they accept – perhaps by reference to national examples –

that sponsorship can work. They will want to know how much they will get for their money and what the tax implications, if any, will be. A club can offer publicity for the sponsor's services or products at their sports ground or in the foyer of a local hall. Their name can appear on your advertisements. Certain sporting bodies allow the sponsors' names to appear on sportswear. Being the only or first team in a league to tie up a sponsorship deal should ensure local publicity for both you and the sponsor even if only for the novelty value.

Club members as the sponsor's patrons

The club can also deliver its members to the sponsor. This is not meant to be taken literally but all other things being equal, there is no reason why your members should not patronise the sponsor rather than anyone else. This can be by the club recommending the sponsor or giving the sponsor access to the club membership list. The financial services industry – insurance brokers, building societies and banks – are always interested in access to new clients. Tell a potential sponsor about your members – their age range, their marital status, their income levels and so on. A club with lots of young single people could be good news for a mortgage broker or an estate agent. Within a short time, many will be out househunting. Other sponsors may specialise in services for elderly people. The deal can be further cemented by a sponsor giving a discount to your club members or agreeing to increase sponsorship by reference to a percentage of the amount your members spend. The first method is less fuss for the sponsor and is directly attractive. Members can simply get a discount on the production of a membership card. But the second method is more use to the club. It is probably more suited to sponsors selling high price items such as houses and cars.

Because the name of the sponsor and club will be intertwined, it is as well to ensure that the sponsor's business will not offend club members. Obviously no brewery would sponsor a temperance organisation but what about the local supermarket? That sells alcohol too. The sponsor's interests could also clash with those of one or more club members. That may not rule out the deal but it shows the need to take care.

Prepare realistic estimates of what it will cost the sponsor or your club to change your posters, buy new football shirts or give the sponsor space in a programme. Try and project forward for a few years. Research shows that it takes time for a sponsor's name to become fixed to an activity or club. Ensure that your prospective sponsor understands this. Many national bodies controlling sports and leisure activities can help you with case studies and other back-up material.

Never forget that sponsorship is not charity. It is not a donation. It is a payment by a business for promoting the business name, products or services. It is a commercial deal. It is not philanthropy. At its crudest, it is selling advertising space on the shirts of a football team. You will need to be ready to spell out the finance and tax considerations to the prospective sponsor.

Tax

Sponsorship is treated by the Inland Revenue as a payment which can be deducted in computing business profits for tax purposes – provided it is of a revenue nature (and not a capital payment) and is incurred wholly and exclusively for the purpose of the trade. If the payment does fall into this category, then the sponsor will save tax at the corporation tax rate, currently 27 per cent or 35 per cent for larger companies, or if the sponsor is a partnership or sole trader at the highest applicable rate of income tax. The ability of partnerships and sole traders to deduct sponsorship payments from their taxable profits is especially important to local leisure organisations. Over the past few years, most professions including solicitors, architects and accountants have allowed their members to advertise. The great majority of professionals work as partners. Outside the biggest partnerships, few have advertised in any way. Many would welcome the chance to gain local exposure.

AMOUNT OF SPONSORSHIP

There is no upper or lower limit to sponsorship. On the local level, it is worth stressing the lack of a minimum amount, as many potential sponsors might be put off by the multi-million deals reported in the national media. But whatever the amount, the expected publicity benefit from the sponsorship should be reasonable in relation to the amount. And that means that a six-figure sum, however generous the sponsor may be, will in all probability not be allowed for tax relief if it goes to a club of two hundred members. It is important to remember that if the sum appears to go beyond advertising expenditure and becomes a donation – perhaps satisfying a director's personal whim – the whole of the sum can be disallowed for tax relief and not just the portion over and above the real promotional expenditure.

In these circumstances, it is best to arrange for two separate sums to be paid. The waters can be further muddied if part of the sponsorship deal involves giving the sponsor entertainment facilities at the clubhouse restaurant. Here again, it is better from the tax point of view if a specific and separate payment is made. But this need for care with the Inland Revenue should not detract from the publicity value of sponsorship. If the total value of the deal under all headings – promotion, entertainment and donation – adds up to £10,000, then this is the figure that the local press should be given. That is the true measure of the sponsor's generosity towards you.

Sponsorship cash cannot generally be tied to capital programmes such as building a new clubhouse or constructing a new arts centre. Such projects would normally be disallowed for tax relief.

VAT

If your club is registered for VAT, you will have to charge VAT at the standard rate on sponsorship cash but not on a donation. The VAT authorities use much the same definition between a sponsorship deal and a donation as the Inland Revenue. If you fail to charge VAT at the time the cash is handed over, you will be faced with the choice of either asking for the tax from your sponsor or having the sum treated as VAT inclusive. VAT inclusive means you will have to hand over $3/23$rds of the sum in question.

If your organisation is too small to be registered for VAT, then there will be no need for any addition of VAT. This sounds like stating the obvious but it has implications. Potential sponsors of your club that charge standard rate VAT on goods or services can deduct the VAT they spend on sponsorship from their VAT bill. The same applies to companies which sell zero-rated goods such as books. They can sometimes end up with a refund. Companies in these two groups do not care whether they pay out VAT or not. For if they are charged VAT by a VAT registered club on a sponsorship payment, they can reclaim it.

Exemptions

But there is a third group; VAT exempt companies and firms. These are mostly to be found in the financial services area and would include banks, building societies and insurance brokers. They cannot claim back all of the VAT a club charges (although they can offset it against their corporation tax or personal tax if they are a partnership) because of the complexities of VAT legislation. They would, therefore, prefer to deal with a club which is not in

the VAT net, provided, of course, it met the other criteria
for sponsorship.

Other means of help

Businesses can help you in ways other than simply handing
over cash. Providing services is one method. Local printers
may want to print your programmes and tickets at cost price
or less. A local garden centre might find it worthwhile
maintaining your grounds. The variations are endless.
If the goods or services are provided at a loss then the
difference between the charge and the cost price to the
provider can be treated as a sponsorship payment by the
provider. Other companies may wish to second staff to you
for a few hours a week though they cannot claim the cost
against their own tax bill unless your club is a charity.

ATTRACTING SPONSORSHIP

Sponsorship generally works best from the taxation point of
view when it is used to finance revenue items. Sponsors
should therefore be encouraged to give a once-a-month sum
for the maintenance of a stand (with their name on) rather
than a lump sum which would enable the club to build a
new stand. If they do the latter, it may massage their
corporate ego but not their corporate accounts. But the
dividing line between tax-deductible sponsorship and a
donation, if it exists, is extremely fine. As each case has to
be judged on its merits, there are no universal rules and
ultimately, the decision rests with individual tax inspec-
tors. The ideas to encourage both sponsorship and
donations in this chapter and the next are not intended,
therefore, to carry any particular tax implication.

Methods to persuade people to part with relatively small
amounts of money might not just be applicable to small
companies and partnerships but also to individuals who
cannot, of course, claim tax relief. And certain clubs have

found that it is better to approach local business people as individuals. They appeal unashamedly to the ego of their targets and many have found that business people whose companies do not bear their own name prove to be more receptive. Other local worthies such as town councillors are also worth approaching but there is no harm in offering certain 'sponsorship' deals to the members themselves. The listing of a member's name on a wall plaque 'in perpetuity' in return for a fixed minimum donation can work wonders. A seat with the donor's name on a plaque is a commonly used fund raising method for theatres and similar organisations.

Where to put the sponsor's or donor's name needs to be considered. Besides plaques on seats, there is advertising in the club programme, on the scoreboard, around the perimeter of the ground and providing equipment and especially matchday equipment which wears out (such as balls). Bigger clubs might consider offering the sponsor/donor advertising space on the players' shirts. This can be extended to shirts, pullovers and sweatshirts for non-playing members. Many will be quite happy to walk around with the legend 'XYZ Industries supports the ABC Club' particularly if the garments are well made. The interests of neither sponsor nor club are served by poor quality merchandise. Other goods such as mugs, ties and pens can also be customised in this way and sold to members. You can often push sales of these items upwards when they mark something special such as a club team winning a cup, a new facility opening or an important anniversary.

BANK LOAN

If your club raises a bank loan, a company may wish, as part of a sponsor agreement to stand as a guarantor to reassure the bank that somebody will pick up the loan repayments if your club does not. If the sponsor is called upon to make a payment under the guarantee scheme, there are certain circumstances when the sponsor can claim a capital loss. As the rules are complex, professional help is needed before any such arrangement is finalised.

AVOIDING TAX

Donations to charities can be arranged so that the donor obtains tax relief but as Chapter 11 shows, only a minority of clubs, societies and other organisations can qualify as charities. Sports clubs and leisure organisations are rarely charities although clubs with a religious or educational purpose could be. To stay out of the VAT net, a donation must be given unconditionally and it must not attract any publicity (other than the acknowledgement of the donation in a programme or annual report), facility, benefit or preferential treatment. If it fails to meet any or all of these criteria, it will be regarded as sponsorship and VAT will be chargeable. And don't forget, it is the duty of any club in the VAT net to insist on VAT when it is due.

You have to be aware of the publicity and tax implications for a potential sponsor so that you can sell the scheme to a firm which might never have thought of the idea before. But you need to do more in selling your club. You will need to be flexible. If a sponsor wants to support an event which has always been run on the last weekend of May but has a new product coming out in mid-June, be prepared to change dates or risk losing the deal.

It is a waste of everybody's time applying to companies for cash a few weeks before you need it. They will probably think you are in a panic and reject your application as one coming from an organisation of incompetents. But even if they don't, they may be unable to help you as the publicity budget could already be tied up. Allow a year between starting your sponsorship quest and (hopefully!) finalising the deal. Find out who is in charge of publicity in the company you target. Write to them as well as the chief executive. Both sides benefit if you agree all deals in writing. A verbal promise of funds is not good enough.

Be honest in what you offer. If your membership is one hundred and you normally attract fifty to any one occasion, tell the sponsor the real figures. Sponsors would rather know exactly how many are receiving their message and tailor it to suit rather than be disappointed by a low turnout. Work out with your sponsor whose responsibility it is to contact local and specialist press with an announcement and agree the wording of the press release. Otherwise chaos will ensue and both you and the sponsor will have missed a chance of free publicity.

Finally, never look upon sponsorship cash as a basic source of revenue for your club. It is the icing on the cake.

7 Fund raising

Fund raising must be related to a club's stature and needs. A jumble sale will not be appropriate for a large club with substantial property and a large membership. It is unlikely to raise enough to make more than the lightest dent in the club's overdraft or more than the slightest improvement to the building fund. But it can be worthwhile for smaller clubs. Equally, very small clubs are unlikely to be anything but embarrassed by the response to a grand gala ball at the city's best hotel.

Professional fund raisers

But before listing any fund raising ideas, a word of warning. There are scores of professional fund raisers on the charity, voluntary organisations, sports and social clubs circuit. Some simply try to sell you products such as lottery tickets, games machines and ready made 'mini-fairgrounds' for a summer fête. They are selling you a service. You pay for the goods and make of them what you can. You will need to consider their suitability for your club but you can always check the prices they quote by going to a competitor. Many printers can quote you for lottery tickets. The various magazines such as *Club Mirror* and *Club Secretary* which cover the commercial aspects of running a club often carry advertisements for all sorts of fund raising gadgets, games and other ideas.

There is, however, a second form of fund raiser. And that is someone who takes the whole or part of the job away from you in return for part of the amount raised. They often claim to be able to raise huge sums. And sometimes they do. But often they work on the basis that the club gets nothing until their own costs including often equally huge personal fees are covered. Some clubs and charities have found that although the amount raised may double or treble using professional fund raisers, the cash that actually goes into their coffers is well down on their previous home-grown activities. The reason is simply that club members do not charge for their own efforts leaving the club to bear no more than the costs of printing, postage, phones and petrol. Even less scrupulous fund raisers have simply disappeared with all that they have raised. So while the majority of professional fund raisers are reputable, be careful.

If you do decide to use a professional fund raiser, contact the national body for your activity to see if there is anyone they recommend. Personal recommendation is perhaps even better but wherever you get a recommendation from, make sure that you see written records of past ventures especially those in similar situations to your own. Also ensure that you get a clear picture of who does what, and information on the financial situation of the fund raiser. It is essential to agree that all incoming funds are put into a special account which the fund raiser cannot have access to without the club's permission. And try to insist that at least a proportion of the fund raiser's earnings are linked to success. If very little is raised, then very little should be earned.

Many clubs offer a 'Vice President's Club' allowing members and outsiders to become vice presidents in return for a fee which may cover them for life or for a number of years. It is purely honorary, of course, and the vice presidents can have no effect on club policy. It is worthwhile putting an upper limit on the number allowed to give the feeling of exclusivity although this number should not be so low as to discourage applicants. Special

badges, ties or scarves can be supplied – with their charge
perhaps built into the cost of becoming a vice president.
Reserved seating on special occasions can also be offered.
Many clubs have been successful with an annual dinner for
vice presidents and their partners, who tend to come from a
homogeneous age and social group. Being a vice president
need not be passive, however. Clubs often find that anyone
committed enough to pay the extra annual fee to become a
vice president tends to be zealous in activities such as fund
raising and getting publicity for the club.

Family membership

Family membership is often attractive. It should be pitched
at around two and a half times the full individual
membership. It can be especially worthwhile if your club
serves alcoholic drinks as the prohibition on the presence of
children under 14 that applies in public houses does not
extend to bars in registered club premises. Many parents
like a lunchtime drink at weekends and resent having to
drink in a pub garden or in a special 'family' room – and
many pubs offer neither. They may well be attracted to club
membership on those grounds if no other.

Hiring out club facilities

If your facilities are of a good quality, they can be hired out
for parties such as children's birthday parties or wedding
celebrations. You could do a deal with a local caterer or
entertainer and thereby provide an 'all-in' service but this
could have VAT implications. If you can provide at least
beer and sandwiches, you may be able to hire the clubhouse
to local businesses holding sales and other conferences.

Carrying out projects through the members' labour not only
effectively brings in money (or at least saves you from
having to spend it), it can also help foster a better spirit

between members. There is nothing like working together in manual labour such as building and maintenance work to improve the feeling of togetherness. Where the skills exist many clubs have 'self-built' facilities. A large club will find that all the skills needed in building a pavilion are likely to be found among the membership.

Fêtes

Summer fêtes are a good idea if the weather holds. Again, it is a way of using the enthusiasm of your members. Some equipment such as roundabouts can be hired from specialist concerns. Other 'fairground' items can be made by members and stored from year to year. The weather can prove to be a dampener. You can insure against rain but not against other forms of bad weather such as heavy cloud or cold. If possible, it is worth having your summer fête in an area where there are alternative indoor facilities so if the weather is cold, you may still be able to salvage something. If you have never held a summer fête or similar event before, look through the local newspaper one year ago for the week in which you intend to have your event. That way you will be able to judge the extent of the competition. Try to avoid having your event on the same day as one that has been around for years, is professionally organised and has high prestige otherwise you may find that not even all your members attend. There are only a limited number of summer weekends and that figure is reduced still further by holiday weeks. So you are unlikely to have the field to yourself.

Jumble and car boot sales

Timing and weather can also have an effect on jumble sales and car boot sales. The last few weekends before Christmas and the month of August are off-season for these in many parts of the country, again the local newspaper will provide guidance. Assuming you have premises for a sale, you could always try when others are unwilling. The most you can lose is your time. Jumble sales remain popular in both rich and poor areas. Helpers should be allowed to have a limited 'first refusal' on the goods donated which are often of a high quality and eminently resaleable. If you feel that a jumble sale is beneath the dignity of your club, organise it in the name of a section of the club such as a junior section if you have one. Teenagers and children like selecting, sorting and selling jumble – although they must always be supervised by a responsible adult.

Car boot sales depend much more on good weather and your possession of a suitable car park either near to other car parking or close enough to a shopping or residential area that people can walk to it. The normal practice is to charge less for car owners who book space in advance. They will only get their money back if the sale has to be called off. Car boot sales, however, are not the attraction they once were. In a substantial number of areas there are too many, and they are often of poor quality. It is also hard to prevent the sale being taken over by professional market traders selling goods of dubious origin or safety standards from the back of a van.

Sponsored events

The 'sponsored' activity is also worth considering especially if you have a major project as a target or if you are a charity. Almost anything with distance involved such as swimming, running (the so-called 'fun-run' rather than the sub four minute mile), walking and cycling can be sponsored. Others have tried weight reduction and periods of silence. But as sponsored events are so common, you will need to do something unusual to gain press coverage – perhaps a version of the 'triatholon' which involves swimming, running and cycling.

Sponsored events need a lot of organising and, especially if young people are involved, a lot of supervision. Road events such as walking or cycling should have a lower age limit. A number of sponsored events have come under fire by safety authorities and the police. If you do organise something on the road, make sure there are plenty of stewards patrolling the course in cars ready to rescue anyone in trouble.

Take the advice of the local police who will tell you if there are places to avoid. Provide all those taking part with instructions on dress, footwear, the route and the need to present a 'clean' image of the event and the club. Neither participants nor organisers are allowed to collect money *en route* unless they have the relevant licence.

Although the task to be sponsored should not be too soft, don't set absurd targets for the participants. Many givers offer a fixed sum and will happily give £2 whether at 20p per mile for 10 miles or 10p per mile for 20 miles. Make sure that the sponsorship forms are well laid out and emphasise to participants the need to collect money as soon as possible. If your participants are adults, ensure that an entry fee is paid as some will be taking part simply for the exercise and will not be interested in collecting cash. Half-marathons and sixty-mile cycle rides often attract thousands of adults from a wide area so ensure that there is plenty of pre-event publicity. All those who take part should end up with a certificate detailing their achievement.

Avoid events that will attract criticism. Eating races where the participants try to eat as many pickled onions in a set time are not everyone's idea of a suitable event in the light of world famine. A sponsored event will do nothing either for fund raising or the club's image if it is criticised in the local press. Promoters have to gauge feelings beforehand, remembering that an offensive event does not become less offensive because it is raising money for a good cause.

8 Gaming

It comes as a surprise to many club treasurers and other committee members to learn that the law governing the club's bingo session derives from exactly the same legislation as that controlling West End of London casinos where high rolling habitués think nothing of staking £100,000 and more on a single spin of the roulette wheel. And that is the Gaming Act 1968.

That is the bad news. The good news is that this act and subsequent legislation brought a large measure of common sense to the previously chaotic state of the law on gaming activities which are regarded as innocent amusement by some yet excite strong moral objections among others. The law now only applies a light hand on clubs organising events which might be construed as gaming or gambling. The club, as a private entity, can allow what might be best described as 'a certain measure of small scale gaming' on its premises without seeking licences or other forms of permission as long as the gaming is confined to club members and their guests. Life becomes much more complicated when outsiders are allowed to participate or when the stakes start to rise.

While, as we shall see later, lotteries and certain other forms of gaming can be organised to help boost club funds, gaming activities on club premises should firstly be seen as an added attraction of the club rather than a way for the club to make money. Clubs that hope to raise large amounts from gaming face additional rules and requirements.

The essential rule to remember is that the club must continue to act as a members' club. Seen informally, the intention of the law relating to gaming in clubs is akin to that relating to drinking in clubs. The controls are light as long as the activity is confined to members and their guests, when it is largely considered to be a private affair. Once outside those constraints, the club effectively becomes a gaming club or casino. The law in relation to both drinking and gaming is concerned to prevent the privileged status of clubs being turned into a method of attracting the general public.

The law on gaming can be complicated and a full exposition would take up several volumes. This chapter is concerned with setting out the basic do's and dont's in order to stay on the right side of the rules. These are the points that a club should remember if it wants to take the simplest possible attitude to low level gaming.

1. Gaming only occurs when something of value is staked.
2. There are games of skill and games of chance.
3. Some games are regarded more seriously by the authorities than others.
4. There are special rules covering bingo and fruit machines.
5. All players must have an equal chance.
6. There must be no hint of private gain.
7. Lotteries are permissible without formality within certain constraints.

There is no law against the playing of any games for 'fun'. If people want to play cards and simply keep a score or if they play roulette without either paying for the chips or gaining any value from them at the end of the game, that is fine.

Gaming law is not concerned with games of pure skill. Cricket, snooker, darts, chess, football and draughts are all considered games of skill. Members can bet on the outcome of a football match among themselves although in some cases this has developed into illegal bookmaking. Roulette, bingo and chemin de fer are obviously games of pure chance with no skill. Amusements such as dominoes, bridge, backgammon and cribbage do involve skill but they also involve a measure of chance as a player's opportunity is increased by a good hand or by the lucky roll of the dice. No matter how much your club's top class bridge player may protest, a game has to offer equal chances to all participants before it can be considered as a game of skill.

'SERIOUS GAMES'

The law differentiates between games such as roulette, craps, poker, blackjack, baccarat and chemin de fer which attract high rolling gamblers and those which, for social reasons, have tended to measure stakes in pennies rather than thousands of pounds such as cribbage, dominoes and whist. Playing 'serious games' at a club generally requires licensing under the Gaming Act. This can be expensive, complicated and involve the police. It is only likely to be viable for clubs where 'serious' gaming is an important, if not the main, attraction.

While a licence virtually confirms your club as a casino, there is a second stage permit known as a 'certificate'. This is much easier to obtain and is only usually refused if the club has less than 25 members or is of a temporary nature. This is similar to the rules governing registration for alcoholic drink. There are rules governing the 'bank' and the need for 'equal chance' so that clubs with a certificate are in effect generally limited to whist, bridge, cribbage, dominoes and backgammon although certain forms of pontoon and chemin de fer are permitted. A club cannot charge more than £2 a day for the facilities provided and all money staked has to be returned to the players. Certification allows clubs to attract members who are interested in the above games and who wish to stake reasonable amounts.

BINGO AND FRUIT MACHINES

Any club organising regular sessions of bingo which are intended to raise cash will need to consider one of the several forms of licence available. The most ambitious clubs which see bingo as a major money spinner will need to apply for a 'cut-down' version of a full gaming licence known as a 'Bingo Only Gaming Licence'. Bingo can also be organised if the club has a certificate although certain forms of bingo – and especially the 'snowball' where a proportion of the cash staked goes forward from week to week – are not permitted. Clubs have to return all stakes to players, making their money from the admission charge and from any refreshments sold.

A club which organises bingo for 'fun' can escape any need for licensing if it conforms with Part 1 of the Act (see below).

Fruit machines are also regulated but here the club can get some advice from those who supply and maintain the machines, for such people have to be licensed under the Gaming Act. In general, a club that is not licensed for gaming – and this means the great majority of clubs – cannot have more than two machines if it does not wish to go further than registration with the local magistrates.

A club can offer limited gaming facilities without any additional permits, licences or certificates if it keeps within Part 1 of the Gaming Act. Any game played has to offer an equal chance to all players. This rules out any game where there is a 'bank' as by definition the 'bank' has a better chance of winning. The club cannot make a charge for participating in such games, although provided that this form of small scale gaming is allowed for in the rules, a club can charge up to 10p a day for admission to a room where the games are played. This charge can be raised to £3 a day for bridge and whist provided no other gaming takes place other than fruit machines. The idea is to provide social amusement and not serious gaming.

The Part 1 rule is a narrow definition designed to protect clubs wishing to offer low key dominoes and whist drives. But a club can, under certain circumstances, organise other games provided that the stakes are low. And that is gaming as entertainment not held for private gain. The effect is to allow a small scale game of roulette – or something similar – to be played at the club's annual dinner. In fact, the rule can also apply to less formal entertainments providing that any gaming is subsidiary to the main purpose of the club on that occasion.

The rule insists that there is no 'bank', that all players have an equal chance, that only one payment be made in the course of the occasion and then not more than £1 and that the total value of all the prizes (whether cash or goods) must not exceed £100. The proceeds – cash taken less prizes and expenses – can either go into the club's funds or be given to charity.

LOTTERIES

Lotteries fall under three headings: small, private and Society. The 'small' lottery is one which often takes place at a social function under the heading of 'tombola'. The tickets can only be sold during the main entertainment and all proceeds less expenses have to go to the club. Prizes must be goods, not cash although a voucher such as a book token would be allowed. Clubs organising such events usually find that many local companies are willing to donate prizes.

A 'private lottery' is exactly what it says. It is restricted to members of the club and the lottery can only be advertised on club premises. Tickets must bear the name and address of the promoter and indicate the fact that sales are limited to club members. Any good printer who offers lottery tickets will be able to advise on the correct form of words. Cash prizes can be offered. All the proceeds must be devoted to the club.

But the best money raisers are 'Society's lotteries' which enable tickets to be sold to the general public. Clubs cannot run more than one week or 52 in a year and all proceeds must go to the club. There must be no private gain. The drawback is the need to register with the local authority and to send in a return analysing the proceeds to the authority. Very large lotteries looking to raise cash of over £5,000 must be registered with the Gaming Board in addition to the local authority. The Board charges for registration and can examine the accounts of the lottery. Profits from such a lottery are subject to Corporation Tax although this could be reduced with careful planning.

9 Alcohol

Taking the decision to sell alcoholic drinks by opening a bar on your premises is one of the biggest decisions that a club can take. It is a move that must be carefully thought out. And before coming down for or against the idea, it is best to set up a special sub-committee to investigate the matter and your members' views on it.

There are three major plus points in opting for a bar:
1. It can be a money spinner. It will attract the cash your members might otherwise hand over to the local pub.
2. By adding a social attraction to the club, members get more involved both with the club and with each other.
3. The club can attract members who are interested in the social aspects of a bar rather than the activity for which the club was first set up.

But there are some disadvantages:
1. It will add to the complexity of the club's bookeeping.
2. You may need cash and space to set things up.
3. You will have to become involved with the licensing authorities, the police and the fire brigade.
4. Some members may object.
5. You may encounter a problem with security. You will have to make arrangements to secure large amounts of cash overnight. You will have to find somewhere to secure expensive drinks such as spirits. And whether you employ bar staff or get your members to work behind the bar, you will have to watch out for the danger of stealing from the cash register.
6. You could become responsible for dealing with the

effects of alcohol. Fights and vandalism are far from unknown. And there is the problem of drinking and driving.

Most clubs find the advantages outweigh the disadvantages and provided they have suitable premises, they open bars. Before you do so, however, carry out some market research. Announce the possibility loud and clear to your members. Ask them what they think of the idea and how much they would use the bar. Once you have collected their views, halve whatever they say. They are not deliberately lying but experience shows that whatever initial interest there is soon declines to a more sustainable level. The early days of any venture have a novelty value. And members of your club are more likely to say what they think you want to hear rather than what they really think.

Look at the alternatives for your members. As a club bar, you have one disadvantage over other facilities and two advantages. The drawback is that your premises are unlikely to compete in style or luxury with the smart new winebar on the high street or the redecorated pub in the suburb. However there is no reason why the club bar should be a slum. On the plus side, the laws governing club bars allow you to open your bar to children under 14 who are banned from public houses. This can be a big attraction if your members have children, especially at a weekend lunchtime.

Breweries
But the biggest advantage you can offer is that drinking in a club is much cheaper than in a pub or winebar. And in addition to a saving on every drink they buy, your members know that the profits go back into club funds which are used for their benefit. Drinks in a club are cheaper than elsewhere because clubs usually use their own clubhouse – there is no need to pay additional rent and rates, the

barworkers can be (but not necessarily) members from the club so that you save on wages (although you should budget for free food and drink for your volunteer force) and breweries are very keen to make you loans for equipment purchases at very low rates of interest which fall as the volume of beer sold goes up. Brewing involves a high degree of fixed costs so that once a brewer has passed a certain sales target, each extra pint is almost pure profit. It is these additional pints that often go through club bars. This should enable club and brewer to come to some mutually satisfactory terms. Don't be afraid of entering discussions with more than one brewer.

Once you are signed up with a brewer, you cannot serve any one else's beer. Most club treasurers find this an advantage as it cuts down on the paperwork. The bar staff will also find it easier and there is far less chance of wastage than if you had to open several barrels of beer from different brewers. You should also get technical and marketing help from the brewer who will probably also supply wines, ciders, soft drinks and mixers to you. Your volume sales of these drinks are unlikely to be enough to make it worth shopping around. A deal with a brewer offers much. The alternative go it alone strategy will usually mean less profit for the club.

RUNNING THE BAR

At the planning stage, you will have to decide whether to employ someone to run the bar. Volunteer labour is cheap but a good bar steward could save you money by his full time presence. He will do some of the less interesting cleaning jobs that many volunteers sidestep – jobs that may be essential if your club is not to run foul of the health authorities.

It is only worth considering employing a steward if the bar is to be open at normal club times. If, as many clubs, you decide to open only at weekends, you are unlikely to find it economic to employ someone, as part time work generally means casual bar staff or staff that claim to be permanent but who stay just a few weeks. Such people are counter productive.

Bar stewards commonly expect accommodation at or near their place of work. Providing accommodation plus the wages and other costs such as national insurance can easily work out at £250 a week which a steward would have to earn by a mixture of saving and increasing sales. But do not forget that members working behind the bar will take a few free drinks. And that they are not in front of the bar, buying drinks.

Legal Requirements

Once you have made up your mind that the club bar will prove to be profitable and you have come to at least a provisional agreement with a brewer, you now need to consider the legalistics of obtaining permission to set up a bar. If your club is a members club – that is a club where all the members have an equal share which ceases when they leave the club – you need to apply for a registration certificate under section 40 of the Licensing Act 1964. You may consider it worthwhile discussing your application either with a lawyer who specialises in such matters or, and this will save money – with a legal expert from the brewery.

Next, apply to the magistrates court. Objections can be made by almost anybody. The police can oppose your application if they think it will become the haunt of criminals or prostitutes, be used for indecent displays or be conducted in such a way that disorder can ensue. The fire brigade can object on safety grounds. The local authority can object on planning and amenity grounds. The police, fire brigade and local authority can all inspect the premises under various Acts of parliament. Additionally almost anyone else among the general public including potential rivals in the drinks trade can object for almost any reason. A suggestion that you will be supplying alcohol to non-members is damaging while a failure to have more than 25 members will ensure that your bid to open a bar is turned down. Very small clubs are considered to be no more than excuses for secret drinking dens. If your application is rejected, the court has to inform you of the reason in writing.

Those are some of the negatives that can prevent your club's registration – the club equivalent of a licence. But assuming your club does not fall foul of any of the above, there are also some positive arrangements you need to make before you can obtain the registration document. Some will entail changing the club's rulebook.

MEMBERSHIP RULES

The first is the 48 hour rule which is designed to stop clubs issuing instant membership tickets to anyone who wants a drink. This states that at least two days must elapse between an application for membership and the grant of membership facilities – or if membership is issued instantly, the member must wait two days before being able to use the bar.

You also have to show that you are a genuine club. As well as having a minimum of 25 members, you must have an elected committee to supervise the bar – this applies whether you employ outside bar help or not – and it must be the club as a whole that makes the profit on the drinks and not an individual, a company or a group of members to the exclusion of others. That applies to all the drink sold on the club premises. You could, if you wanted, franchise out the supply of food in a club restaurant. You could come to an arrangement with a caterer who might supply the food and give the club a fixed sum per month whether the restaurant was profitable or not. But you cannot do that with the supply of alcoholic drinks.

You will have, of course, to satisfy the magistrates that you have made arrangements so that only members can buy alcoholic drinks. The normal practice is to have membership cards and for members to sign in non-members as guests. The guests cannot buy drinks as legally the purchase of drinks in a club is not a sale but merely a transfer of cash to the club in return for a drink from the club. For while the drink is still in the barrels and bottles, it belongs to the members. When a member wants to drink it, he or she effectively reimburses club funds. It is as if the club was selling off old sports equipment.

Members only is one of the most important rules to enforce. Failure to do so could result in your registration renewal being turned down. And if there is an objection from a member of the public (possibly a local publican!) before that – the court can order the revocation of your club's registration. Ignorance of this rule is no defence and the effect on your club's finances and your club's standing of losing the right to sell drinks will be catastrophic. A number of notices should be displayed to point out that your bar is for 'members only'. Many clubs insist that membership cards be shown before a drink can be purchased.

There are some exceptions to this rule to allow visiting members of other clubs to buy drinks provided that your club rules allow them to enter the premises other than as guests of your own members. This relaxation applies to ex-service clubs, most workingmen's clubs, clubs of similar learned, educational or political objects or when a nearby club has to be closed temporarily for repairs or renovation. It is also possible for the club to hire out its bar to an outside body – for a party perhaps – and to keep the bar open in the normal way, serving those connected with the outside body. This can be a useful way of raising funds but local magistrates will not look kindly on clubs which offer this facility too often. The definition of 'too often' is unclear and many magistrates will put a ceiling on the number of such occasions each year. However, the exact number will depend on local circumstances.

Your club will have to undertake certain formal requirements. You will have to maintain an up-to-date list of members and specify which serve on the club committee and which serve on the bar committee.

OPENING HOURS

Clubs are not exempt from the general rules affecting opening hours. They must be stated in the club rules. Clubs cannot steal a march on the opposition by opening earlier or closing later than other drinking establishments in the locality. Licensing hours are under review at the time of writing – and those in Scotland and Northern Ireland are quite different – but currently club bars cannot open for longer than 9½ hours on a normal day or 5½ hours on Sundays, Good Friday and Christmas Day. There must be an afternoon break of at least two hours on normal days and on Sundays and the two religious festivals, the bar cannot be open for more than 3½ hours after 5pm. Ten minutes are allowed at the end of each session for 'drinking up'. A club may apply for a 'special hours' certificate if it has a good reason to vary these hours. A club appealing to night workers might well qualify. There are special rules regarding hours for clubs which supply substantial meals with drinks.

If you want to have live music and dancing, you will have to apply for a separate certificate.

As a club, you are exempt from the rules which prohibit the entry of children into public houses except in areas specially designated such as 'family rooms' or 'gardens'. Because the supply of alcohol in a club is not a sale, the rules preventing the sale of alcohol to those under 18 does not strictly apply. However, it would be seen by the magistrates and the police as grounds for the refusal or the revocation of the registration. If your club allows under 18s into full membership, your club rules will have to make it clear that adult use of the bar is prohibited until members reach the age of 18.

But despite the nature of the supply of drink to club members, the club cannot escape the legal requirements of the Trades Description Acts and other acts of consumer protection. It is illegal to serve short measures or to pass off one drink as another. Unless indicated otherwise, sherry must be Spanish; port must come from Portugal. And the only sparkling wine you can refer to as Champagne must be real Champagne. The same applies to Cognac. Terms such as Italian champagne or Spanish cognac are illegal in the United Kingdom even if they are used in certain countries.

This chapter is intended to provide general guidance and is not an exposition of licensing law. You should consult a suitably qualified professional for further clarifications. The law as stated in this chapter does not necessarily apply to Scotland.

10 Raising a loan

Clubs can either raise cash for expansion through their own efforts or through a loan or a grant. The first course involves convincing the members while the second necessitates convincing professionals who deal with requests for capital all day long. Your members will need convincing but they may be prepared, in their enthusiasm, to overlook the odd weakness in the club committee's case. Financial professionals will not and cannot ignore flaws in your plans. They will expect you to come to them prepared with all the facts and figures and ready to answer the most searching questions. Many cost their time at £50 or more an hour. They will not be happy spending their time discussing an ill-prepared case.

A potential lender will want to know:

★ Who you are and what your experience is, both in business generally and in the club in particular.
★ What the club is, its purpose, its membership details and how it has evolved over time.
★ Financial figures for the past three years if possible, up-to-date details of the current financial year and projections.
★ How your internal accounting system works.
★ Details of any other borrowings.
★ How much you want.
★ Why you think you can succeed against local competition.
★ How you intend to pay the loan back.
★ What security you can offer the lender in case the project fails.

★   If you and the committee are prepared to offer your own
    assets as security.

Back of envelope 'accounting' will just not do. Your written
presentation is the first impression you will create. In some
cases, that will be sufficient for the potential lender's
decision making. Around one in five of all investment
plans submitted to financial institutions are rejected at a
very early stage. Often, there will have to be a meeting
with the lenders. You will need to create a good impression
because they will be looking to you for eventual repayment.

Don't forget that whether lenders have sympathy with your
club's objects or not, they are duty bound to be interested
in nothing more than your ability to pay back the loan and
the interest due on it on the agreed dates. A second point
to remember is the better the security, the lower the rate of
interest.

If you approach a brewery for a loan, they will want to
know all the above information but also how your plans will
sell more beer and other drinks for them. Brewery loans are
usually structured so that the rate of interest falls as the
number of barrels of beer rises.

Important bodies worth approaching for possible grants and
aid in finding friendly lenders are the Sports Council
(16 Upper Woburn Place, London WCIH 0QP and
regional offices throughout the country), the National
Playing Fields Association (25 Ovington Square, London
SW3 1LQ), the national body for your particular activity
and the various tourist boards.

In event of being turned down

If you receive a negative response at your first attempt, do
not despair. Once you have examined the causes for your
failure and you have rectified any weaknesses in your

presentation, try elsewhere. All available sources should be reviewed including banks, building societies, financial institutions such as finance houses and organisations that offer grants such as the Sports Council, local authorities and the various tourist boards. The offer of a grant from an organisation which is well known for its stringent vetting of applicants may well persuade other lenders to join in. You should, however, be prepared to accept cash help at a lower level than your initial plans demanded. The committee should discuss whether a smaller loan should be accepted – and the project trimmed to suit – or rejected.

While a loan is the normal method of raising cash for a substantial project especially one that involves property, any club thinking of buying a particular piece of equipment but which is unwilling or unable to borrow cash might consider leasing as an alternative to purchase. Leasing entails renting the item for a specific period of time with the option to purchase the asset at the end of the leasing period for an often nominal sum. Leasing uses the tax system to reduce the payments as these are fully allowable against tax. It is not classed as borrowing so it would have no effect on other loans. The rental payments are fixed unlike many forms of loan where the rise and fall of interest rates can affect the most sophisticated cash flow projections.

Raising money for leisure activities is a difficult process at the best of times and it is even more problematic when a club committee functions only in its members' spare time. Raising money has to be approached in a totally business-like way. The committee has to be ruthless with itself, throwing out any plans with too many 'ifs and buts'. A lender or a grant-making organisation is looking for as near a waterproof cast iron case as possible. They are not rich benefactors or patrons. The days of such people are largely over. You must have a firm financial base to start with and present an excellent case.

11 Charity

Charity is standing on a windy street corner waving a collecting tin under the noses of passers by, sending money to help combat hunger in the third world or the victims of some disaster nearer home and helping the poor without thought of personal reward. But there is more to charity than that. For beyond the usual understanding of the work, it has a more precise meaning. And if your club, or part of your club, can fit within the Charity Commissioner's definition of the word (the Inland Revenue's in Scotland whose views do not necessarily coincide with those south of the border) then there could be a number of financial advantages including tax relief and lower rates.

What is charitable status?

But before any club treasuer gets too excited, it is necessary to point out that very few sporting or social clubs will successfully be able to apply for charitable status if they merely duplicate or substitute commercial facilities. The social club which revolves around the bar will be seen as no different from a pub while the golf club is not essentially any different from a commercial concern with a golf course, other than in its mode of ownership. These clubs can no more apply for charitable status than the purely commerical companies running pubs and leisure centres. These clubs as well as the local angling society or the pub darts team exist solely for the benefits of their own members even if a lot of voluntary work goes into their efforts. In effect, they are typical clubs: a grouping together of individuals to enhance the quality of the lives of those individuals.

HOW TO CHECK IF YOU QUALIFY
To qualify as a charity demands more. The problem with applying for charitable status is that there is no rule book defining what is and what is not a charity. The law governing charitable status is generally regarded as hopelessly muddled while there is a substantial degree of public concern over the large number of charities that are several years behind on their returns to the relevant authorities. Thousands of charities have disappeared without trace.

There are, however, four tests which are generally quoted and if your club fits into any of them, you could take the matter further and consult a lawyer to see if it is worth applying for charitable status. The four pointers are:

1. The relief of poverty.
2. The advancement of education.
3. The advancement of religion.
4. Other purposes beneficial to the community.

In addition, under the Recreational Charities Act 1958, it is charitable to provide leisure and recreation facilities such as sports and village halls for public use. Such a charity must be for the public benefit and in the interests of social welfare.

Within these definitions, there is obviously substantial room for debate. The second and fourth points are the most applicable to clubs. Offering free or low-cost facilities to young people would help with an application under the second heading as would the creation of scholarships, the awards of certain trophies and prizes or the offer of club expertise to local schools. But merely promoting the activity to the young may not be enough so a campaign to encourage more young people to play croquet may not be considered charitable but the offer of practical advice including lessons to those who could not otherwise afford it might well be approved. A club that could extend those guidelines towards the community in general and more especially the old, the infirm, the poor and otherwise disadvantaged of both sexes could also apply under the fourth heading.

Whilst a club's activities as a whole may not satisfy the charitable tests, part of its activities such as a youth section may qualify if established as a separate entity. Clubs must decide here as elsewhere whether the advantages of setting up a separate entity repay the efforts involved.

The charity would normally have, as its object, that of improving the conditions of life of those for whom the charity is intended. Indeed charitable status will not be available unless the club can demonstrate that it is established for charitable purposes only. To do this in a way to satisfy the relevant authorities entails substantive references in the objects of the club. It could be argued that a poetry society which gave free readings to the general public was charitable on this basis but that a cricket club which offered free admission was not.

Effect of being a charity

DISADVANTAGES

But even if a club can fit itself within one of these interpretations of charity, there are other legal hurdles. The first is that the payment of a subscription to use facilities disqualifies a club from being a charity. This means that if a club is involved in social or educational work, it must set up a separate arm as the charity. The second is that a charity cannot refuse membership to any individual in the way that a club can. The third is that the legal costs of setting up a charity are unlikely to leave much if any change from £2,500.

However, often a solicitor member who is willing to be co-opted to the committee may be a useful source of free advice. Before charitable status is effective, the club must be registered with the Charity Commissioners and the Inland Revenue.

ADVANTAGES

Once over these hurdles – and possibly others, as the above is of necessity a thumbnail sketch and not a legal guide – there are a number of positive benefits. The first is rates relief. Local authorities have the discretionary power to allow clubs in general up to 50 per cent rates relief. Whether they do or not will depend on factors such as public access to facilities, the availability of the club to local schools, the degree of profitability of ancillary services such as a bar, whether those profits are used for the purposes of the club and the overall financial state of the council. Many local authorities will use their discretion in such a way that only part of the club premises are accorded rates relief. The bar and restaurant at a club may not qualify but the area in which the activity takes place could. What many local authorities do in effect is to work out their own definition of a charity and apply that to clubs in their area whatever their status. But a charity has to be accorded at least 50 per cent rates relief but at the discretion of the local authority, the degree of relief can go up to 100 per cent.

Tax

Charities enjoy substantial tax advantages. They neither pay tax on the surplus of income over expenditure provided it is not trading, nor on capital gains. And donations to a charity are exempt from Inheritance Tax – assuming the charity has wealthy friends who are prepared to leave it money for its purposes. The charity can also arrange for its supporters to sign deeds of covenants which commit the donor to giving a fixed sum for at least four annual payments. The charity can claim the basic rate of tax on covenanted income back from the Inland Revenue. On a basic tax rate of 25 per cent every £75 donated will produce £100, on a basic rate of 27 per cent, it needs £73 to produce £100 while a 30 per cent tax rate only needs £70 to benefit the charity with £100. Charities are losers when tax rates fall.

Furthermore, if the individual pays tax at the higher than standard rates, additional tax relief will be available. In the case of someone paying tax at a top rate of 50 per cent when the basic rate is 25 per cent, £25 will be refunded to the taxpayer for every £100 of charitable donation producing a net cost to the individual of £50. Meanwhile the club will still receive £100.

If no longer a charity

Charitable status is lost if the charity ceases to have charitable aims. Your club may, for instance, decide that it no longer wishes to be involved with education. In practical terms, the charity should seek to distribute its cash as soon as possible in accordance with its aims. If these aims have ceased to exist, then it has to distribute the cash to an organisation whose aims are as close as possible to those of the charity. What usually happens is that a charity hands over the money to a regional or national organisation with similar aims. The relevant authorities should then be notified.

12 Tax

Each year the government takes many hundreds of millions of pounds out of sport and leisure by way of taxation. Value added tax is levied on club subscriptions, theatre and sport admission tickets and on just about everything else connected with running a club except gas and electricity. Income tax and national insurance are also levied on the many people directly and indirectly employed in sport and leisure.

The exact amount the government receives from sport and leisure are not available though estimates put it as high as £1.7 billion. But two things are clear. The government does not give back, via national and local arts and sports funding bodies, anything like the amount it takes out. And although many do not realise it, tax can affect the running of all sorts of clubs. Dealing with tax is a duty of the club treasurer, who may be held personally responsible for the amount due as clubs, unlike limited companies, have no legal status. But while the treasurer has a duty to pay any tax due from activities of the club, there is an equal and obvious duty to the members to minimise the burden as much as possible. There is no exemption even if, as with most clubs, the whole object is to further a recreation activity and not to enrich either individuals or even the membership as a whole. There are no special tax reliefs or incentives. And some that did exist such as the allowances on money spent on plant and equipment have been reduced over the past few years.

Many clubs and societies escape all taxes. Most are too

small or are run on such a shoestring that there is never any money around for the Inland Revenue to take. Others are clubs which are effectively closed circuits. The money going in comes entirely from the members and expenditure is equally entirely devoted to the mutual interests of the members. Such clubs escape the tax net as all that is happening is that a group of people have joined together to spend some of their personal cash collectively. This is known as Mutual Trading and clubs in this category are of no interest to the Inland Revenue unless they receive income from interest on a bank or building society account or if they sell an asset such as land or a building. But once, as we shall see later, mutual trading reaches a certain threshold, such clubs are liable for VAT.

In general, thinking about tax is an essential from the day the club is established. For even if there is no immediate tax liability, the treasurer will have to monitor events very closely as the club could easily slip into the tax net. Problems can start at some clubs when the annual subscription is collected especially in the sort of club that provides lavish facilities in return for a high annual subscription. More modest organisations may find they have a tax liability as soon as they provide services such as a bar and individual sports facilities for which members have to pay each time they take advantage of them.

Clubs that provide services for non-members or which charge admission fees for certain events are also liable to be caught in the tax net. Clubs that employ people either full- or part-time will have to account for tax and national insurance. Additionally, companies and individuals donating money can also run into tax complications.

What kind of tax?

There are two golden rules for treasurers to remember. They must record all transactions in an efficient way and be up-to-date. Equally, any treasurer who is uncertain on any point should contact the relevant tax authority as early as possible. The Inland Revenue (income and corporation tax), HM Customs and Excise (value added tax) and the Department of Health and Social Security (national insurance) tend to be far more sympathetic when doubts and difficulties are brought to them earlier rather than later. Finally, don't be afraid of seeking professional help from an accountant. That can save many months of agony!

CORPORATION TAX

If your club is in the tax net, it is likely to encounter corporation tax. Corporation tax is to organisations including clubs (whether formed as companies or not) what income tax is to individuals. For all but the very largest clubs (defined as those with profits over £100,000), corporation tax is levied at 27 per cent – the same rate as basic rate income tax. It has been the government's policy for some time to align the rate of corporation tax on small companies with the first tier of income tax. Tax is payable on the profit on any income received from non-members and the income from the investment of any previous profits made from areas such as the bar which were raised in the first place entirely from members. The income from any fund raising activities such as lotteries and sales is taxable if cash is received from non-members as will almost certainly be the case. Cash received for sponsorship whether from companies or individuals is a grey area. As a basic rule, it can be treated as taxable income if it is given in return for services including publicity and not as a pure donation.

Clubs need to be especially careful with investment income. If they keep their spare cash in a bank or building society in a deposit account (or other similar account which pays interest), the interest will be paid with basic rate income tax deducted. Individuals cannot reclaim this tax whatever their personal tax position but under certain circumstances, clubs may be able to use it to offset other corporation tax liabilities. Some special accounts aimed at club treasurers pay interest without any deduction of tax.

Corporation tax is payable on the net sum of interest received turned into a gross sum. If the club receives £75, adding back the basic rate income tax ('grossing up') if the tax rate is 25 per cent produces £100. The £25 deemed to have been paid on that interest is offset against the club's corporation tax liability. If the tax is higher than the liability, any excess is repaid.

Income

PROPERTY

If the club lets out property it can deduct certain costs from the rents received. Insurance, repairs, maintenance, rates and mortgage interest are all allowable expenses but if that produces a loss, it can only be offset against profits from other property and not from other trading. Expenses connected with trading such as wages, heating and lighting and transport can be deducted from income. In theory, such expenses have to be 'wholly and exclusively' for the purpose of trading but in practice, the Inland Revenue may be able to agree to relief for a reasonable proportion of expenses when that spending was only partly directed towards the trading activity. Heating and lighting the clubhouse, for instance, would rarely be exclusively for trading activities. Don't forget that even the club jumble sale counts as trading.

LAND

Many clubs own land. Some may have invested in stocks and shares or been given these or other assets by benefactors. If they are sold, corporation tax is levied on the capital gain. This is calculated by subtracting from the sale price the original cost plus a factor to cover inflation since 1982. If that results in a loss, the minus figure can be carried forward indefinitely to be offset against a future gain. If any substantial disposal is made, it is usually worth engaging professional help as there may be opportunities to reduce the tax bill.

CAPITAL GAINS

A capital gain can arise from an insurance claim. If a sports building valued at £10,000 is burnt down and the club is reimbursed by its insurance company, there could be a capital gain or loss depending on the original cost of the building. But if the capital raised through an insurance claim or a sale is reinvested into facilities for the club, no tax is payable. What happens is that the gain is subtracted from the cost of the new asset. If land is sold for £50,000 creating a capital gain of £20,000 and all that cash is used to buy a clubhouse costing £50,000, the Inland Revenue assumes that the clubhouse only cost £30,000. If it were sold for £100,000, the gain would be £70,000 less an adjustment for inflation. Reinvestment does not abolish the need to pay the tax. It defers it. To do this successfully demands following a number of detailed and complex rules including the need to invest all the proceeds from the sale (you can of course add more) and to do this between one year before and three years after the disposal.

Employment

A club that employs anyone will have to make arrangements for income tax to be deducted from the wages of employees under the Pay As You Earn (PAYE) system and for national insurance. Substantial amounts of back tax are collected each year from clubs which have not complied with their obligations.

SELF-EMPLOYED

Problems arise in deciding just who is employed and who is self-employed. As the self-employed make their own arrangements for tax and national insurance, it can be attractive to be classed as self-employed. The dividing line between the two is thin and often confusing but while full-time work will usually put that worker into the employed category, part-time work does not equal self-employment. One test is to see the degree of control over the job that the person carrying out the work has.

Someone who comes when necessary to repair the snooker tables is probably self-employed. The repairer works to his own timetable, can leave as soon as the repair is carried out and presumably works in a similar capacity for whoever wants this type of work. But a part-time barperson would almost certainly be employed. He or she would have to attend during the agreed hours whether there is work to do or not.

CASH PAYMENTS

It is tempting to pay such a person in cash and hope – although not necessarily believe – that he or she will make a tax return. If they do not, the Inland Revenue may look to the club for the tax. And the Inland Revenue can go back six years – more if fraud is suspected. The tax people will treat the cash payment you made as a net payment. If you pay someone £50 in their pocket, it will gross that sum up by adding on the standard rate of income tax and then tax the club on that amount. The club ends up paying much more than it bargained for. Unpaid national insurance is collected in much the same way.

Expenses

Clubs may reimburse genuine expenses to members who are involved just for 'the love of the game' without incurring a tax bill. These expenses could include the cost of travelling to matches and other events at a reasonable rate such as second class rail travel or the Automobile Association mileage rate for cars in the 1,001 to 1,500 cc class and the cost of special individual equipment such as football boots and training gear. But once the amount paid is more than the simple reimbursement of expenses, the whole sum and not just the excess becomes taxable. The individual becomes classed as an employee.

PAYE

The treasurer will also have to make returns under the PAYE reporting requirements. Treasurers who have neither the time nor the inclination to immerse themselves in the mysteries of PAYE might find it easier to hand the whole job over to one of many agencies which specialise in this work. The cost will be more than recompensed by the knowledge that the club will have discharged its responsibilities to its employees, to the Inland Revenue and to the Department of Health and Social Security.

13 VAT

Value added tax – VAT – is controlled by Her Majesty's Customs and Excise. It is a tax that is quite unlike the taxes on profits and capital gains which are under the aegis of the Inland Revenue. The latter organisation is interested in taxing profits. If your club merely breaks even or loses money in a year, then there will be no tax to pay even if you have to fill in a return. VAT is unconcerned with whether you make a profit or a loss. It is a tax on activity and turnover. If your club has an annual turnover of £50,000 and profits of 50p, the Inland Revenue will not be interested, but the Customs and Excise will. Alternatively, if your annual sales of £10,000 generate a profit of £5,000, you will receive a bill (more properly known as an assessment) from the Inland Revenue but it is unlikely that the VAT authorities will be concerned.

It is unusual in a second way. Large profitable organisations can end up either paying no VAT at all or even enjoy a rebate of the tax each quarter. Any VAT-registered concern can reclaim all the tax paid on goods purchased, known as inputs, and subtract that from the tax charged to customers on outputs. A business whose output is zero rated – a newspaper publisher or a manufacturer of children's clothes for example – would find their input tax is greater than their output tax and therefore they would qualify for a rebate.

It is important to keep accurate VAT records and to file returns and pay any tax owed promptly. New severe regulations have been introduced which penalise any business that sends in returns and payments even one day late. You are advised to obtain proof of posting if you send your returns in near the deadline. Postal delays are accepted as an excuse provided you have proof.

Who has to pay?

All businesses – and as far as VAT is concerned all clubs and associations with certain exceptions are considered to be businesses even if they are not run on especially business-like lines – have to register for VAT if their annual sales are over £21,300. This is the limit for the tax year 1987–88 and the level is usually raised in line with inflation at each budget. But there is a second test for VAT registration and one that is very important for clubs. Unlike corporation tax which is calculated on a yearly basis, VAT is assessed on a quarterly basis. A business with a turnover in any three consecutive months in excess of £7,250 (1987–88) has to register for VAT. This means that many clubs such as sports clubs whose activity is very seasonal have to register even though sales on a yearly basis are below the annual limit.

Besides smaller clubs, organisations of political, religious, philanthropic, philosophical or patriotic nature are also exempt from VAT registration provided that the basic subscription covers no more than an annual report and accounts and the right to know about, attend and to vote at meetings. But if any other benefits of membership are supplied, the whole organisation falls into the VAT net. Other benefits would include free magazines and news-letters, free advice and information, the provision of social activities and meetings at which 'guest' speakers appear. Of course, if the benefits fall below the VAT level, no tax is payable. Some organisations of this nature may find it more convenient to split their works into two of which only the second is run as business subject to VAT. However, HM Customs and Excise might not allow this arrangement and end up subjecting both parts to VAT. It is essential to obtain professional advice before making such a move.

REGISTRATION

If you register, you have to charge VAT (the standard rate is currently 15 per cent) on all sales, including membership subscriptions, which attract the full rate. You can register for VAT when you are still below the limit although in general it is rarely advisable to do so if you are more than a few thousand pounds under the level. You will not be allowed to register for VAT if you turnover is substantially below the level. There are facilities for deregistration if your sales continually fall short of the VAT limit. The current deregistration threshold is £20,300.

STANDARD AND ZERO RATED FACILITIES

Most club activities including sports facilities, entertainments and the provision of food and drink (both alcoholic and non-alcoholic) are standard rated. Certain activities are zero rated. As far as clubs go, the most important zero rated items are magazines, books and other literature (but not records and tapes or stationery) and certain types of cold food (excluding most forms of confectionery) which is supplied to be eaten away from club premises whether by members or non-members. The word 'premises' does not just include the bar or restaurant. It takes in the surroundings. Food or drink supplied from the bar which is consumed around the edge of the cricket pitch, for instance, will be standard rated. If it is removed uneaten and taken into the street and then consumed, it will be zero rated. Most food and drink supplied by clubs will be standard rated. The club's turnover in both zero rated and standard rated goods counts towards the annual registration limit.

There is a third form of goods and services known as 'exempt'. These not only carry no tax but do not count towards the annual or quarterly limits. Two important areas for clubs which are exempt are sports competitions and betting. A fee charged to enter a sports competition is exempt provided that the fee is levied by a no-profit making sporting body or if all the cash raised by the entry fees is returned as prize money to competitors. The amounts staked in lotteries, bingo games, fruit machines and certain other forms of gaming are also exempt and fall outside the VAT net. But the cost of printing tickets, buying or hiring fruit machines and admission fees for bingo sessions are liable for VAT.

How to pay

Once you are within the VAT net, you must keep comprehensive records of all the VAT you pay for goods and services you receive – known as your input – and of all the VAT you charge on services and goods which you sell. The second amount is called the output. VAT is normally collected once a quarter. Towards the end of each three-month period, the treasurer will receive a return which is simple to fill in. Essentially, all that needs to be stated on the form is the amount of input tax paid on goods and services purchased and the amount of output tax charged to customers. Subtract the greater from the lesser. This will usually result in your organisation owing VAT, so send off your cheque with the return. You always have one month to do this after the end of each quarter.

However, from the middle of 1988, VAT accounting will be simplified for small businesses – defined as those with an annual turnover of taxable supplies of under £250,000. Provided that a club or business has had at least one year's satisfactory record paying VAT, it can then move over to annual accounting. In that case treasurers will have to make just one annual return instead of four. Clubs and other businesses that agree to go over to this voluntary scheme will sign a direct debit payable to the HM Customs and Excise which will take nine equal payments based on an estimate from previous trading. There will be a tenth balancing payment to pay – or a rebate to collect – when the annual return is submitted.

Although this will save treasurers a certain amount of time some will prefer to keep to the old system as the quarterly payments exert a considerable discipline. A second reason that a few treasurers will find for preferring the old system is that it can aid cash flow.

A second new option open to small businesses with a good VAT record is cash accounting. Small is again defined as an annual turnover of less than £250,000. Normally you pay VAT at the end of each quarter on all amounts that have been invoiced in that period whether that invoice has been paid or not. If you have a slow payer, you will have to pay the VAT due. If that slow payment turns into a bad debt, you will be able to reclaim the tax but the method is long and cumbersome. With cash accounting, you only pay VAT when you receive your money.

But there is another aspect to cash accounting. Under the conventional method, you can reclaim input tax in the first return after you receive an invoice from your supplier whether you have paid the bill or not. If you can manage to spin out payment, you have an obvious advantage. Cash accounting does away with that. You can only reclaim input tax when you have paid for the goods.

Annual accounting offers positive advantages to many clubs. It simplifies cash flow as well as saving on administrative time. The value of cash accounting to a club is more doubtful. It offers no advantages whatsoever to a club which gives no credit. And most clubs with their mixture of bar takings, fees for facilities and membership subscriptions fall into that category. Cash accounting does, however, offer considerable advantages to any club which hires out facilities and finds that the hirers are none too prompt in paying.

However you pay, you must ignore all exempt goods and services. The normal pattern is for your output to be higher than your input. But if the main thrust of your sales were in zero rated items such as books and publications, you could find the output tax you collect less than the input tax you have paid to suppliers. You would then collect a refund from HM Customs and Excise. Don't forget that this has nothing to do with profitability although your profit and loss figures will have to take account of the ins and outs of VAT. Your accounts may also be of interest to a VAT officer.

Membership fees

Membership fees are normally standard rated but it all depends on what services are provided. A social club whose main purpose was music and drinking would have to levy VAT on the full membership fee. But a club which supplied nothing other than literature to its members would find that the membership fee could be zero rated because it relates to the supply of goods that are zero rated. An organisation which supplied both could apportion the subscription between the two. Suppose a club's turnover was £50,000 a year and – because the treasurer keeps clear books showing how the club's sales break down in categories – £10,000 of that was for the provision of zero rated (or exempt) services and goods, then one-fifth of the membership subscriptions would be equally zero rated. While there are no specific rules for apportionment, your calculations will have to be available for inspection by a VAT officer. They will not allow apportionment if the amount claimed is trivial. Your local VAT office or your accountant will help you if you need further advice.

Reducing VAT

VAT is essentially a tax on the final user of the goods or services. If you can stay out of the VAT net, it will help your members. Your members will save on membership fees and on goods such as sandwiches as the bread, butter and cheese, cooked meat etc., are zero rated items in a food shop. They will save less on goods such as alcoholic drinks which already carry tax. You will not, however, have to levy VAT on the mark-up between the price your club pays for a bottle of beer and the price it charges members. One way of staying below the limit is to break the club up into separate constituents. For instance, a sports club with an annual turnover of £30,000 could divide up into a cricket club, a football club and a tennis club – all of which would be below the limit. This solution could be more trouble than it is worth as each club will now have to have separate books, separate bank accounts and separate meetings for members.

OUTSIDE EVENTS

A second method of keeping the club's turnover below the VAT line would be to arrange certain events outside the club. If the club holds an annual dinner for 200 people at £20 a head, that would amount to £4,000 or nearly one-fifth of the annual level and over half of the quarterly figure. If an outside restaurant or hotel organised the occasion and payment was made directly to that outside caterer, that is £4,000 that does not go through the club's books. The drawbacks are that the club would lose out on the profit on catering and the members would have to pay VAT at the outside location. But it could save them from VAT on other activities and the club could negotiate a small commission for each dinner ticket sold.

DONATIONS

Some sensible planning can take many charges that the club may make for admission to events out of the VAT net. The easiest method is to pass the collection box around at half-time or the tea interval. This form of voluntary donation – and the voluntary must be stressed as there must be no coercion and no suggestion of a 'correct' level of donation – is not subject to VAT. Donations are outside the scope of VAT whether a formal admission·charge has been made or not. Fund raising events can be priced so that the cost of the food, entertainment or whatever else is provided is separated from the donation element. If your amateur dramatics society holds a gala presentation of its latest production and charges £10 a seat compared with the normal £2, then provided that the balance of £8 is clearly labelled as a donation, it will escape any VAT.

PROGRAMMES

One method put out by some as a way around VAT is the expensive programme. In the past, many organisations have charged a pound or more for a programme of one page which alone gives admission to the event.

Programmes, these clubs argued, were publications and were therefore zero rated. The affair was even more clouded as clubs at one time used admission programmes rather than tickets to get around restrictions on Sunday entertainments. VAT officers now look at the substance and intent rather than the outward signs. If the programme is being sold for £2, they would look for a value in the programme alone similar to other publications at that price level. A club could contest the findings. But it is rarely likely to be worth the time, effort and cost to defend a programme that does not have a substantial amount of reading matter and anything that does is likely not to be a programme but a magazine. As HM Customs and Excise always start off regarding a programme as standard rated and as no club has·

yet successfully contested this, it is a VAT-reducing method to avoid. It does not work.

Looking ahead

It is well worth thinking about VAT before your club gets to the annual or quarterly levels. A sudden improvement in the affairs of the club can push you over the limit very quickly. The Customs and Excise has the power to recover VAT which should have been levied but which was not. You, however, will not be able to recover the VAT which was not paid by your members or their friends. In addition, you may have to pay penalties. These penalties are up to 30 per cent of the VAT that should have been charged or £30 if that is a greater sum. Current indications suggest that these penalties are being rigorously enforced as are other penalties for late payments and failure to keep records for at least six years. This follows a period when huge amounts of VAT-registered traders were lax in their returns. At one time, it was estimated that over £1.2 billion was outstanding in this way. Further new penalties designed to tighten up on VAT traders are being introduced progressively between now and 1989.

It is normal practice for a VAT officer to visit your premises and inspect your books around a year to eighteen months after you first register for VAT. This is intended as an opportunity to correct any errors in your VAT accounting methods as well as a check to see that tax is not being evaded. After that, visits are at random, usually every few years.

14 Insurance

Most clubs belong both legally and morally to their members. That is fine as long as the club progresses. But even in a well-run club, there could be occasions when something goes terribly wrong. There could be a fire or a theft which would diminish or wipe out the value of the members' assets. Even worse, the club could find itself on the receiving end of a huge claim for negligence of one sort or another. And as any one perusing the press recently may have noticed, courts are awarding tens if not hundreds of thousands of pounds in response to proven cases of negligence when serious injury is caused.

Unless a club is well covered by insurance, such claims could end up as personal liabilities of the club committee or the club members depending upon the actual structure of the rule book. Insurance is essential and it is as well to start off with a good insurance broker. Only registered brokers can use this title and most will be members of the British Insurance and Investment Brokers Association (formerly known as the British Insurance Brokers Association). Avoid those who describe themselves as 'insurance consultants' or other similar titles. They may possess neither the expertise in the insurance market nor the professional indemnity insurance to protect their clients against their mistakes. A list of members of the BIIBA in your locality can be obtained from BIIBA, 10 Bevis Marks, London EC3 (01-623 9043).

Good brokers will tell you if they are interested in your

business and whether they feel capable of handling it as some brokers specialise in other fields of insurance such as life or motor. Your broker is obliged to tell you the rate of commission on each policy provided you ask. Some brokers will share this with the club if the club gives the broker some form of advertisement. The broker may be able to offer a cut-rate group scheme in areas such as private medical insurance if a certain number of your members sign up. The club's broker could be mentioned in the annual report or co-operation in mailing publicity material to members. The return of part or all of the commission in return for a service such as advertising normally counts as taxable income in the hands of the club.

In conjunction with your broker you will need to analyse every aspect of your club's life and decide what needs insuring. You need to bear in mind that damages whether awarded in court or from out of court settlements are growing in our increasingly litigious society and that as a result insurance rates are soaring even faster. Sports field injuries and injuries to spectators caused by on-field activities were once covered by the legal principle of '*volenti non fit injuria*' which loosely translated means that people who willingly take part in an activity cannot claim damages if an incident that is likely to happen in that activity causes them injury. An obvious example is a footballer breaking a leg.

But that legal principle has come under fire in recent times and is not the watertight defence it once was. The footballer with a broken leg might blame a badly prepared pitch or claim it occurred as a result of illegal play by an opponent. Allegations of assault by opponents in games such as rugby are growing. Personal injuries tend to be the most expensive potential risk faced by a club.

Your broker will draw up a list of risks under a maximum of four categories: liability, benefits, contingency and damages. Liability covers injury or death to persons or damages to their property caused by the direct or indirect actions of your club. Injury from a falling rooftile at your clubhouse would be covered as would the greenhouse window broken by an errant cricket ball. You may also have to take out insurance to protect the facilities you have hired from an organisation.

You should ensure that the insurance is drawn up in such a way as not to exclude club members and the committee itself. Public liability insurance is not expensive and even if a court decides that a club member cannot sue the club, the time, expense and worry of fighting such a claim is just not worth it.

EMPLOYERS' LIABILITY

If you employ people – even on a part-time basis – you must as a matter of law possess employers' liability insurance. You may also need to arrange life cover for them as well as pension benefits although this will be by negotiation. Any vehicles owned by the club must be insured to the minimum standards required by the Road Traffic Acts although higher levels of cover are normal. It may not be enough for members to say that they are covered to drive any vehicle.

Damages insurance for the club's premises include many of the items you would insure for your own home such as cover against fire, flood and theft. You will also need – depending on the size and scope of the club – cover against deterioration in food and drink stocks, special theft cover and perhaps social precautions if you have valuable cups and shields and insurance against staff dishonesty.

LOSS

Clubs with a licence to serve drinks can also protect themselves against the financial effect of the loss of that licence while any loss of profits due to any of the above events such as closure of the club through fire can be covered by a consequential loss policy.

Contingency insurance of varying kinds will cover an event against loss due to varied events such as the weather or the non-appearance of the opposition team.

Many clubs which invite the public onto their premises believe that they can avoid all legal actions for negligence by putting up a notice to the effect that any individual using the club does so at his or her own risk. Such notices no longer have any legal validity. The Unfair Contracts Act states that a person cannot lose the right to sue for damages for injury or death either as a result of a notice or even if they have signed a disclaimer. Many clubs have made guest membership conditional on signing such a disclaimer.

One of the most important factors in insurance is that the more people that can be covered by one policy, the lower the unit cost. Much of the cost involved in personal insurance is administrative. So if you organise a club tour, try to insure your members as a group. Standard 'holiday' cover on a group basis would insure against medical expenses (especially useful outside the United Kingdom) liability of individuals and belongings. Expensive items such as jewellery and cameras can be tricky. You may have to pay extra and insist that each member pays the club as an individual. Alternatively, many members may already be covered against loss or damage to valuables under a domestic household contents policy with an all-risks extension applying, to the United Kingdom and very often the whole of Europe (a geographic entity whose identity varies from company to company). A group policy would also insure the club against the loss of specialist equipment. The medical and accident section of the policy may need special negotiating if the club's activity is one such as hang-gliding or pot-holing which are normally excluded from standard insurance policies. This may take time so give your broker plenty of notice.

MEMBERS' PERSONAL INSURANCE

It should always be made clear to members that with the exception of specific insurance such as cover for a club trip abroad or where the club is using bulk purchasing to reduce the price for individual policies, the insurance purchased by the club does not mean that members should stop buying their own. In many cases, insurance will cover them only as members of the club and only when on club business. It sounds obvious but each year thousands of people assume they have more insurance cover than they do.

Reducing the insurance bill

There are few risks which are beyond the scope of insurance but no club can afford to insure against any and every possibility such as the breaking of a glass. If you did, you would find that the insurance would cost as much if not more than the item being insured. Equally, some of the items discussed in this chapter may not be applicable to your club. An often overlooked method of reducing your insurance bill is to adopt the 'catastrophe' theory of insurance. This says that if the club loses £100, it is a nuisance but nothing more. But if there is a loss of £1,000, that is a catastrophe and the club will have to pack up. So you structure your insurance, if you can, so that you only claim if your loss is large. That will reduce your costs, in some instances by a dramatic amount. Don't forget that many brokers will be happy to share some commission with you or 'throw in', free of charge, a low-cost insurance item such as public liability in return for the names and addresses of your members. Tell your members if you make any such arrangements so that they know why they are getting promotional material from the broker.

Once you have drawn up your insurance shopping list with your broker, the next stage is to see if any of the items are covered by insurance bought by the national or regional body for your activity or if those bodies have negotiated any special deals. Check through a valuable publication *The Insurance Buyers Guide to Schemes, Packages and Unusual Risks* (published and updated annually by Kluwer Publishing) to see if there is anything else you should consider. This book is available in public libraries and many insurance brokers have a copy. It is the source of the information in Appendix II.

15 Safety

'**N**o one ever gets hurt in a sports or social club.' 'Our major activity is playing bridge and surely that cannot injure anyone.' 'Yes, you can get hurt playing tennis, but preparing the courts? Never.' Those are typical reactions from club committee members when asked about their arrangements for safety.

Although it is obviously true that working in a club is a safer occupation than mining, railway work, construction work or being a test pilot, nevertheless, injuries do happen. Bar staff trip over crates left in the wrong place. They could also fall off step ladders when asked to hang up Christmas decorations. They could suffer burns and scalds when engaged in cooking. The ground staff can have all manner of accidents with motor mowers and with chemicals.

Costs

Safety is not strictly speaking the realm of the club treasurer. But because it is a legal and moral necessity – breaches of which can be punished by fines as well as the award of potentially huge damages to those hurt in an accident – it impinges on the finances of the club. Safety falls into two categories. There is the need for a safe environment for employees whether casual or full-time. And there is the equal requirement to adhere to the highest levels of safety in all dealings with members of the public whether they are members, visitors or simply those who find themselves in the vicinity of club activities. All this costs money but these are expenses that have to be considered before any other. It is pointless to spend a vast sum of money on a new clubhouse and then find it does not meet the latest safety legislation.

The club treasurer has to be aware that safety precautions can be expensive and that any project which involves expansion can mean that the club premises as whole move into a different category requiring more stringent precautions. This could entail extra cost in the existing premises.

Legal responsibilities

The club has a common law duty towards its employees to provide a safe working environment. It has more specific duties under the Health and Safety at Work Act 1974. Although there are penalties for breaches of all Health and Safety legislation, the most important aspect of this law and other associated measures is to prevent accidents. Employers must provide advice, information, training, safety clothing and equipment as necessary. The cost of this must be budgeted. The staff must take reasonable care to avoid accidents. If a guard is provided for use on a certain piece of ground maintenance machinery or if protective clothing is needed and supplied for handling certain substances, then the employer must see that they are used.

Many of the measures such as fire safety also apply to users of the club. The number of recent tragedies has led to further reinforcements of the Safety of Sports Grounds Act 1975. The authorities are now examining relatively small grounds whereas once their interest was entirely concentrated on the major sporting stadia. The club has a legal responsibility to spectators and other visitors whether or not it charges for admission and whether or not any charge is called 'temporary membership'.

Remember that under the Unfair Contract Terms Act

1977, simply posting up a disclaimer such as 'This Club takes no responsibility for the safety of spectators' is no longer admissible as the defence in any legal action. However, it is reasonable to assume that a court will take a different view of a spectator hurt at a motor cycle race when crossing the course than of a spectator at a snooker club who is injured when a light fitting falls down.

HIRING OUT FACILITIES

The Act is aimed primarily at sporting stadia and a 'general' certificate is issued when all is satisfactory. But whether your ground needs to be covered or not, you may need a 'special' certificate if the ground is hired out for some other activity such as an open air pop concert or an exhibition. Cost is no defence. Many clubs that have been unable to afford improvements have been shut down.

There is, however, specific provision for tax relief which can be given in certain circumstances for these improvements. That does not help, of course, if the cash is not there in the first place or if the club does not pay tax. Some local authorities have at times offered grants or interest-free loans especially if the facilities in question are shared by the public or if they are used by the local education authority.

In case of accidents

Breaches of practice are first tackled by the Health and Safety Inspectorate in an informal way, assuming they are minor. More serious cases are dealt with by the issue of a formal improvement notice. This will give a date by which the improvements must be carried out. Improvements this serious will normally necessitate the spending of substantial amounts of cash. In the most serious cases – or if other measures have failed to bring any improvement – the offending club or other premises can be shut down. There is also provision in the act for fines and imprisonment.

Clubs have a responsibility to prevent injuries to those living or passing the vicinity of the club. Failure to take adequate precautions will invalidate many insurance policies so that the club and its committee could end up being liable for any damages awarded.

It is impossible to list all the precautions required both inside and outside the club as each club is unique. The local Health and Safety Inspectorate will be happy to advise or to suggest specialist surveyors and contractors. It is, of course impossible to rule out all accidents but a safety aware attitude by the club, its members and employees should prevent most. Members and employees should always be encouraged to suggest areas which need further safety work.

16 Disbanding

Clubs come into this world borne on a tide of enthusiasm. Many run into problems along the way and many close their doors. Clubs fail for an infinite number of reasons of which four stand out.

The first and perhaps the easiest to prevent is where a club has been dependent for years on an unchanging committee which eventually through age, change of interest or change of address disintegrates. Clubs should encourage new blood onto committees. Some clubs have a rule banning any member from serving on a committee for more than a stated number of years. Others ensure continuity by insisting that each major postholder on a committee has a deputy.

The second reason for failure is that either the original objects of the club have ceased to exist – a classic case would be an organisation for veterans of a war. Demographic shifts where an area becomes depopulated or where the social make-up of an area changes are also possible reasons for failure. Unless the remaining members can agree on a new course for the club, it will have to close its doors.

Many clubs fail because they are overtaken in the amenities they provide either by other clubs, by commercial enterprises or by competition from other forms of entertainment. Clubs devoted to the showing of 'art' films have suffered from the onset of video recorders. Certain sports have periods of popularity followed by periods of disinterest.

The fourth and perhaps the most common case – and certainly the easiest to avoid – is where a club is forced to close through financial mismanagement. It should not happen if the club treasurer adheres to all the record keeping recommended in this book as this should enable weaknesses to be spotted early and appropriate action to be taken. A club may be the victim of fraud or theft or it may simply be trading at too high a level. Shutting the club bar on evenings in the early part of the week can sometimes help, or raising subscription levels.

Prevention

Club treasurers who spot a problem should bring it to the attention of the full committee immediately. And if there is going to be a difficulty with a loan or with tax, the lender or the taxation authorities should be contacted as soon as possible once the club has worked out the best strategy – taking professional legal and accounting advice where necessary. Remedial action has a better chance of success if it is undertaken early. Bring in professional advisers if the problems seems intractable. It may well be that the club's assets can be used to raise additional capital or that they are underused so that more revenue can be raised. It often needs the appraisal of an outsider to spot this.

How to wind up

But if all the above proves fruitless, the club will have to dissolve. Most model rules include a rule for dissolution. Typically, winding up a club requires a general meeting and the vote of three-quarters of those attending. The rules should also cover the possibility that the meeting is inquorate and that a subsequent meeting is equally inquorate. In those circumstances, it may be left to the committee and any members left to decide what to do. The meeting should also decide where any surplus of assets over liabilities should end up. In theory, they could be shared out among the

remaining club members even though they might have had
nothing to do with their accumulation. In practice, where
there is something over, it normally goes to a central or
regional organisation or to another club in the locality with
similar objectives. If the point is not covered in the rules,
you are still legally obliged to consult all the members.

Clubs run as a company

If the club has been formed as a company, then any surplus
on winding up belongs to the shareholders but again it
would be normal practice for such monies to go to a similar
organisation. They company's articles of association – the
rule book – should make that clear (assuming that is the
wish of the members).

In case of debts

If the liabilities of the club exceed the assets and the club
has not been formed as a company, the committee and
ultimately the membership could be personally responsible
for the debts unless those measures recommended in
Chapter 1 are carried out.

Finally, as most people are aware, taxation follows you to
your death bed and the end of a club is no exception. The
realisation and distribution of assets to club members on a
winding up can give rise to tax liabilities.

Appendix I

Model Club Rules

Every club needs a rule book. But it should not be written in an excessively legalistic or long-winded form. Such rule books offer a field day to the 'barrack room lawyers'. It is a safe bet that any organisation of more than a few people will have one. And in some cases, the very existence of an over-inflated rule book brings out the worst in certain members. However, there can be dangers in having too few rules. For that can lead to chaos or to having rules which are too general, leaving massive power in the hands of the committee.

Rule books are effectively common sense. They should provide the minimal framework necessary to ensure good order. But even the best drawn up rules are no better than the committee whose job it is to administer them or the chairperson who may have to adjudicate. It is their attitude to their task and most importantly the degree to which they are open to members' suggestions and requests for information which determines whether the rules remain as common sense guidance or whether they end up as a lawyers' paradise.

The following rules are intended to be a base to build upon with additional suggestions that might be incorporated into the rules if clubs think it suitable. Almost all clubs will need to alter the basic rules for their own specific purposes. It is always worthwhile asking any central organisation that covers your activity for a copy of their model rules or for any suggestions they may have – especially if you forsee problems. Many central organisations insist that they approve of your rules. This is a pre-condition of membership. The drawback is that the central organisation might have a particularly rigid or an especially bureaucratic attitude to rules. But where there is no insistence on rule book approval, it is always a good idea to get an outsider to take a look.

1. Name and address
This club shall be called the ABC Sports Club. Its headquarters shall be at the Cricket Pavilion, The Park, Anytown.

The name of the club will determine its main activity and how it is seen by the members and by outsiders. If a substantial part of the activities concentrate on the bar, add the words 'and Social' to the title. If possible, have a club address for all communications. Using a committee member's private address can cause complications if that member leaves the club or the committee or is away from home for a protracted period.

2. Objectives
The purpose of the club is to provide facilities for playing hockey, to offer facilities for other sports and for general recreation and to provide food and drink for members and their guests.

It is best to specify firstly the original or main function of the club and then to add in a general phrase so that expansion is not held back by the rules themselves. The above wording would allow the club to change its sporting emphasis to lacrosse or football but not to turn itself into a philosophical debating society. Too wide a definition – such as recreation and entertainment – could allow a group with no real interests in the original aims and objectives to take over the club for their particular activity without gaining whatever majority is laid down in the rules for a rule change.

3. Membership and voting rights
Membership shall be divided into the following classes:
1.   Full members.

2. Family members.
3. Temporary members.
4. Associate members.
5. Honorary members.

1. The rules should contain details of what membership of each class entails. It would be usual for the great majority of the active members to be full members. They should be over 18, and each full member would have one vote at a properly convened club meeting. Only full members shall be able to stand for election to the committee.

2. Family membership is often used as a device to attract membership subscriptions. At least one adult member of each family group should be treated as a full member and if family membership costs more than twice full membership, two adult members could have full rights.

3. Temporary membership is useful for members of opposing teams and for visitors. One and seven day membership is often available but there are no voting rights.

4. Associate membership is often useful as part of a sponsorship deal. if the BBB Ball Bearing Co. gives financial help to your club, it is often a good idea for all employees of BBB to be made associate members by virtue of their employment. They would have no voting rights.

5. Honorary members are those who have performed some service to the club. They pay no subscription but in many clubs have full voting rights. The club must also decide if non voting members have the right to attend annual meetings and if so, whether they can speak. Few will do so anyway.

4. Subscriptions

Members shall pay a subscription as laid down in the annex to this rule each quarter starting on January 1st of each year. Any member joining more than one month after the start of a quarter shall pay either two thirds or one third of that quarter's subscription depending on the exact date of membership. Membership shall cease once a member is overdue by more than x weeks providing that a warning to that effect has been sent to the member's last known address at least three weeks before. Subscription rates shall be decided by a simple majority at the general meeting.

The idea of putting the rates into an annex to this rule is to prevent the revision of subscription rates being turned into a full rule change which needs a 75 per cent majority. Provision for lapsing members is essential. Some clubs may wish to have special rules to cover arrears if the member decides to rejoin. The subscription rule will have to be adapted if the club wishes to attract full life members.

5. Joining and leaving the club

No one shall be elected to full membership without being proposed and seconded by existing full members. Application in writing shall be made at least fourteen days before the relevant committee meeting. No one, whose application is rejected, can be reconsidered before x months have elapsed. Resignations must be made in writing at least fourteen days before the next subscription is due.

All existing full members shall be entitled to know who is being proposed and to object formally to the full committee should they wish. But neither the membership committee (if there is one) nor the full committee should explain to the general membership or to an individual member why they accept or reject a proposed member. The rules should make it clear that no discussion of an individual's membership shall take place at a club general meeting.

Insisting on resignation in writing not only helps with the club's paperwork. It also allows the member to leave without owing subscriptions. If a member resigns formally, he or she should be allowed to rejoin at a subsequent date and be treated as a new applicant provided a set period of time has elapsed. Members who leave without proper notice or who attempt to rejoin before the set period has elapsed shall have to pay arrears.

6. Officers and the committee

The club officials shall consist of a chairperson, a secretary, a treasurer, and a membership secretary. Each must be elected at an annual general meeting and stand for re-election each year. These officials, x other members, elected for three years with one third retiring each year and the playing captain *ex officio* shall form the club committee which will act in the best interests of the club. Casual vacancies among the club officials shall be filled from the committee. The committee shall have the power to set up sub-committees and to co-opt members. Co-opted members shall be allowed to speak at committee meetings but not to vote unless their position has been ratified by the members in general meeting. Casual vacancies shall be covered by co-option. Such committee members shall be eligible to vote but their position must be ratified by the membership in a general meeting. No paid employee of the club, their spouse or their adult offspring shall be members of the committee. No meeting of the committee shall be quorate unless at least one officer and three other members are present.

These rules seek to give the membership the power to vote out the club officials annually while giving the backbone of the committee three years between elections. This should be enough time to 'work oneself into the job'. It also offers continuity. A club with many sections may wish to reserve so many committee places for each section. However, as they would have full committee status, the club will have to decide whether voting is by the whole club or by that particular section on a federal basis. Clubs will work out the size of the committee depending on membership numbers and complexity. Equally rules for a quorum will depend on the size of the committee. Small committees of ten produce tied votes. Clubs will have to decide in their rules whether the chairperson gets the casting vote, whether the **status quo** *takes precedence or whether the matter should be voted on once more at a subsequent meeting. Committees should have rules for their own conduct. These and other important matters should be minuted. Minutes should be made available to members. Where it is necessary, the committee should appoint trustees.*

7. Behaviour

The committee shall lay down standards of dress and other forms of behaviour. The committee shall have the power to discipline any member who deliberately ignores these rules, or who brings the club into general disrepute or who transgresses the rules of the national organisation. The member must be offered a hearing within x weeks of the incident at a time consistent with the club's activities. The member may be accompanied by a friend. The member may be exonerated, reprimanded, fined (not more than £x), suspended (not more than x months) or expelled from the club.

The committee has obviously to lay down standards consistent with the standing and aspirations of the club. Some clubs will wish to lay down that there should be an appeals committee while more rarely others may regard the entire club in general membership as the final arbiter. It would be unusual to return a subscription to a member who has been expelled. Clubs which belong to a national organisation – especially one which allows easy transfer of membership from one club to another – will have to align their disciplinary policy with the national organisation.

8. Meetings

The annual general meeting at which the accounts shall be presented shall be held at 8p.m. on the third Wednesday in April. Three weeks' notice shall be given to all members. The committee has the power to call an extraordinary general meeting at two weeks' notice. The signature of x members (usually 10 per cent and rarely more than 20 per cent) shall also be sufficient to call an extraordinary meeting at two weeks' notice. Members calling such a meeting shall have access to the membership lists but shall bear the cost of any such meeting including that of circulating members.

No meeting shall be quorate unless x per cent of the voting membership is present. The chairperson has the casting vote in general meeting but he or she may not speak in any debate.

Notices convening the annual meeting together with the club's accounts should be sent at least three weeks before the meeting. Some clubs incorporate standard rules for the conduct of meetings into their own rules. These may lay down that no issue raised in one quorate meeting can be raised again until a certain period of time has elapsed. It is customary to hold elections at the annual meeting although some clubs organise postal ballots. Between annual meetings, the committee effectively rules. But there is always the discipline that a minority of members can call an extraordinary meeting and change their decision. Most club rules state that the officers and committee can only be removed on the due date for election. Others allow the removal of individual officers and committee members if three fifths or three quarters of the total membership vote for that course. In those circumstances, anyone not voting is supporting the existing incumbent.

9. New rules

Rules can be introduced, amended or repealed at a duly convened general meeting providing that notice of the intention to alter the rule book is sent out in writing to all members at the same time as that of the meeting. An alteration needs the positive vote of 75 per cent of those at the meeting. Rules should not need changing too often if they are left as sensible guidelines leaving features such as subscription rates to an annex. Some clubs may require that all those qualified to vote are offered an opportunity to judge the issue whether they attend the meeting or not. That means organising a postal ballot.

10. Winding up

A resolution to dissolve the club can be proposed for discussion at an annual or an extraordinary general meeting.

This rule should have the same requirements as to majority and notice as the preceding rule. It should state what happens to any surplus after all debts and other liabilities have been paid.

Appendix II Club insurance

Club insurance 'packages'

See Chapter 12 on insurance.

Ecclesiastical Insurance Group – Clubs Combined Insurance
This is aimed at registered clubs. It covers fire and special perils, public liability, employers' liability, theft and all risks, glass, personal accident, loss of money, consequential loss and loss of registration certificate.

Fielding Smeaton Jones – Club Insurance – cover for fire, special perils, loss of profits, theft, liabilities etc.

Bishop Skinner Northern – Clubcover – insures against property damage, business interruptions, liabilities, personal accident and loss of licence.

Linthorpe Insurance Brokers – Club Insurance – wide range of cover.

Frizzell Bolton Corder – Club Insurance – wide range of cover.

Contingency insurance – cover against cancellation

Adam Brothers Contingency
Lombard Continental Insurance
Prudential Assurance
Sun Alliance Group

Hang gliding and other hazardous sports

Spooners Insurance Services – British Hang Gliding Association Scheme. This offers permanent accident and sickness insurance for the pilots of hang gliders and microlight aeroplanes. Spooners also have a scheme for parachutists and parascenders.

West Mercia Insurance Services – offers travel insurance for individuals and groups with particular emphasis on sports such as mountaineering and parachuting.

Hole in One

The following offer insurance cover against any golfer getting a hole in one which, in itself, would win a prize in a competition. They are also willing to insure clubs against having to pay out on other unusual feats such as rolling seven consecutive sixes in a dice game.

Hamilton & Wellard
John Holman & Sons
Lombard Continental Insurance
Sun Alliance
Herbert Watson Insurance Brokers

Legal Expenses

DAS Legal Expenses Insurance– pursuit of assault and injury claims, disputes with breweries and other suppliers, costs involved in prosecuting 'thugs and hooligans', etc.

Pub Games

Galaxy 7 – Pubs and Clubs Games Operators Risks – covers machines such as one-armed bandits, space invaders and pintables. The insurance protects against accidental and malicious damage and can be extended in suitable circumstances to cover the loss of money content.

Rain

The following insurers provide cover against the loss of income and other costs if more than a certain amount of rain falls during the specified event or – in the case of cricket and tennis – play is not possible due to rain or a waterlogged ground for more than a set proportion of the time set for the game.

Eagle Star Insurance – Pluvuis Agreed Value Policy

Norwich Union – Rainfall Insurance

Sports

Clarkson Puckle Group – Sportsecure. This protects the promoters of sporting and other events against cancellation due to a large number of factors including the weather.

Cornhill – Sports. This covers loss or damage to an individual's sports equipment as well as legal liability and personal accidents.

Entertainment & Leisure Services – provide a wide range of cover for sporting activities including travel.

Galaxy 7 – offers a wide range of policies covering activities ranging from angling to windsurfing including football, cricket, basketball, volleyball, canoeing, hockey, lacrosse, netball and rugby. Cover can be arranged to protect against theft of trophies, loss of equipment, injury to a player, injury to a third party and, by negotiation, other specialised risks. Galaxy 7 will also arrange cover for touring and other travelling by clubs and their members.

General Accident – Bowling Club Policy – This can cover members as well as the club. Usual theft and liability sections are covered and it can be extended to cover damages to the greens and club buildings.

General Accident also has a Family Sports Policy which covers loss and damage to equipment on an individual basis and which can be extended to clubs and associations provided that all the members agree to be included.

W. S. Moody Hilton (Midlands) – Golf Club Policy – covers personal accident and damage to club property.

Tyser UK – provides a number of medical and other policies of interest to sports clubs including touring. It also offers special policies for member clubs of the Rugby Football Union (England).

Names and addresses

Adam Brothers Contingency Ltd, 15 St Helens Place, London EC3A 6AB. Tel: 01-638 3211

Bishop Skinner Northern Ltd, 7-8 St James St, Newcastle upon Tyne NE1 4NF. Tel: 091-232 8682

Clarkson Puckle Group Ltd, Ibex House, 42-47 Minories, London EC3 1HJ. Tel: 01-709 0744

Cornhill Insurance Group, PO Box 10, 57 Ladymead, Guildford, Surrey GU1 1DB. Tel: 0483 68161

DAS Legal Expenses Insurance Ltd, Brigstowe, 5 Welsh Back, Bristol BS1 4SE. Tel: 0272 290321

Eagle Star *see* local phone directory for nearest branch.

Ecclesiastical Insurance Group, Beaufort House, Brunswick Road, Gloucester GL1 1JZ. Tel: 0452 28533

Entertainment & Leisure Insurance Services, PO Box 100, Great Ouseburn, York YO5 9SZ. Tel: 0901 30711

Fielding Smeaton Jones (Agencies), 1 Pepys St, London EC3N 2PL. Tel: 01-488 1488

Frizzell Bolton Corder, Frizzell House, 14-22 Elder St, London E1 6DF. Tel: 01-247 6595

Galaxy 7, Insurance Chambers, 21 Market Place, Abbey Gate, Nuneaton CV11 5UH. Tel: 0203 386022

General Accident PLC, Pitheavlis, Perth, Scotland PH2 0NH. Tel: 0738 21202

Edgar Hamilton + Hamilton & Wellard, 69-71 Great Eastern St, London EC2A 3HU Tel: 01-739 4300

John Holman & Sons Ltd, John Holman House, The Broadway, Wickford, Essex SS11 7AN. Tel: 03744 5566

Linthorpe Insurance Brokers, 1-5 Queens Square, Middlesbrough, Cleveland TS2 1AQ. Tel: 0642 224011

Lombard Continental Insurance PLC, Lombard Continental House, 182 High St, Tonbridge, Kent TN9 1BY. Tel: 0732 362345

WS Moody Hilton (Midlands) Ltd, Tricorn House, 51-53 Hagley Road, Birmingham B16 8TP. Tel: 021-454 7441

Norwich Union Insurance Group, PO Box 6, Surrey St, Norwich NR1 3NS
Tel: 0603 622200

Prudential Assurance PLC, 142 Holborn Bars, London EC1N 2NH. Tel: 01-405 9222

Spooners Insurance Services Ltd, Bank House, 119 High St, Newport, Isle of Wight
PO30 1TP. Tel: 0983 522676

Sun Alliance Group, 1 Bartholomew Lane, London EC2N 2AB. Tel: 01-588 2345

Tyser (UK) Ltd, Acorn House, Great Oaks, Basildon, Essex SS14 1AL.
Tel: 0268 284361

Herbert Watson Insurance Brokers Ltd, Irongate House, Dukes Place, Bevis Marks,
London EC3A 7JE. Tel: 01-623 4811

West Mercia Insurance Services, High St, Wombourne, Nr Wolverhampton
WV5 9DN. Tel: 0902 892661

Index